William Jaroszewski

————————————————Free Yourself in a Business of Your Own

──────────────────Byron Lane

The Guild of Tutors Press
1019 Gayley Avenue, Los Angeles, California 90024

FREE YOURSELF IN A BUSINESS OF YOUR OWN

AN ASTRON SERIES BOOK

COVER PHOTOGRAPH BY HARRY TURNER

CHAPTER HEADING PHOTOGRAPHS BY
HOLLY HARTMAN AND V. M. ROBERTSON

FIRST EDITION

LIBRARY OF CONGRESS CATALOG CARD NUMBER: 78-59917
ISBN: 89615-007-0 (PAPER)

A Note on Personal Pronouns

This book is written for both women and men. Small business ownership is an important way for women to reach absolute equality with men. It is my hope that more women will find the solution to their worklife dilemmas through a business of their own.

I wanted to be clearly non-sexist in my writing, and I tried using he/she and alternating masculine pronouns in one chapter with feminine in another. All my attempts at resolution of the problem were unwieldy and distracting.

My choice is to stay with traditional forms, understanding that they are used generically, not sexually, until such time as we develop a new set of non-sexual pronouns.

To Curtis W. Page, Ph.D.

Without you, Duke, this part of my life would have remained a dream.

Contents

Foreword/8

Preface/11

Part I: Getting Started/13

1. THE NEW ENTREPRENEUR/14
   Classic vs. New Entrepreneur/15—Profile of the New Entrepreneur/16—Evolvement Stages of the New Entrepreneur/18—Businesses Started by the New Entrepreneurs/20—Who Succeeds?/21

2. STARTING A NEW BUSINESS/25
   Business Plan/26—The Business Concept/28—The Management Team/31—Marketing/32—Operations/33—Financial Strategy/33—Getting Free with Little or No Investment/35

3. MAKING THE TRANSITION TO YOUR OWN BUSINESS/35

4. BUYING AN EXISTING BUSINESS/45
   Advantages and Disadvantages of Buying a Going Business/45—How To Find a Business To Purchase/47—Evaluating a Business for Sale/48—How Much To Pay?/49—Making the Decision/50

5. SOURCES OF FINANCING/53
   Equity Capital/54—Debt Funding/55—Little-Known Sources of Capital/58

6. THE FRANCHISE RELATIONSHIP/63

7. FORMS OF ORGANIZATION/67
   The Sole Proprietorship/67—The Partnership/69—The Corporation/70

Part II: Managing the Small Enterprise/73

8. MAXIMIZE YOUR STRENGTHS/75
   Work Your Niche in Life/75—The Advantages of Flexibility/78—Keep It Simple/79—Do Unto Customers/80—The Importance of Specialization/81

9. SMALL FIRM MARKETING/85

Market Research/85—Selecting Locations/87—Product Decisions/90—Pricing for Profit/91—Distribution Through Manufacturers' Representatives/95—Personal Selling/96—Creating a Successful Image/96

10. LOW BUDGET ADVERTISING AND PROMOTION/101

Developing a Program and Budget/103—Newspapers/104—Direct Mail/104—Radio/105—Magazines/105—Public Relations/105

11. UTILIZING THE FINANCIAL STATEMENTS/109

Basic Record Keeping/110—Tips for Simple Record Keeping/111—The Income Statement/111—The Balance Sheet/114

12. CASH FLOW/120

Developing the Cash Flow Forecast/121

13. PLANNING FOR PLEASURE AND PROFIT/125

Whys and Hows of Forecasting/126—Tools of Forecasting/126—Long-Range Planning/127

14. WHERE TO GET HELP/130

U.S. Small Business Administration/130—U.S. Department of Commerce/132—Colleges and Universities/133—Trade Organizations/133—Public Libraries/133—Other Public Agencies/134—Working with Specialists/135

Part III: Working with People/139

15. MANAGING YOURSELF/140

The Process of Personal Growth/141—Translating Personal Growth into Business Results/143

16. MANAGING HUMAN RESOURCES/148

Small Business and the Behavioral Sciences/148—Motivation/150—Collaboration/151—Communications/152

17. SUCCESSFUL EXPANSION/155

The Entrepreneurial Dilemma/155—From "Flair and Hunch" to.Management/156—Shifting Relationships/158—Not Too Fast/158

18. SMALL BUSINESS OF THE FUTURE/161

Small Business and the American Economy/161—Small Business As a Way of Life/162—Small Business as a Force for Change/170

Acknowledgments/173

Index of Photographs/174

FOREWORD

There are many statistics which can be quoted to emphasize the importance of small business in American life. These can be generalized into broad, basic statements, such as "Small business represents approximately one-half of the American economy," or "One out of every two Americans is directly or indirectly related to small business in his economic pursuits and/or life style."

Other facts, such as "Ninety percent of all those who go into small business will probably fail," are sobering in their implications. Those who have been acquainted with small business know of the many hours of work that must be contributed each week, of the seemingly endless personal sacrifices that are required, of the high level of risk, and of the need for "dogged determination," plus more than a "little luck" to succeed.

While these facts reflect the pervasive influence of small business in American life and the difficulties encountered by those who seek success through small business, they do not leave one with any real understanding of the basic appeal and sense of challenge that small business holds for each new generation of Americans.

To understand the meaning of small business, one must look beyond the economic factors to the personal needs of people and to the emotional fulfillment that comes into their lives from being their own bosses, proving themselves, and giving direction to their own destinies. Only when small business is perceived on the emotional as well as the intellectual and economic levels, can its magic spell for millions of Americans be understood.

An essential element in gaining this understanding of small business and of the meaning it holds for people is reflected in the concept of "entrepreneurism." The willingness and the capability of individuals to express initiative in creative ways and to take the risks necessary for success are basic to the thrill and rewards they receive from small business. A number fail in their attempts to establish successful small businesses. Others succeed and are exhilerated by having made it when the ever-present risks along the way were so challenging.

This unique book, *Free Yourself in a Business of Your Own*, approaches small business from a "totalistic" point of view. Through "interrelating work and life," the author highlights the role that small business can play in bringing a sense of purposefulness into the lives of individual small business people, while at the same time it contributes to their economic well-being and satisfies the emotional and financial needs of others associated with the business. Writing in an earthy, appealing style, the author explores with the reader the fundamentals of going into business and the psychic rejuvenation which it provides for those involved.

For those readers who desire to understand and to be more successful in their own small business, for those who wish to gain greater insight relative to the magnetic force which small business holds for people, and for those who are weary of their own personal life styles and who are searching for new meaning and a sense of direction, this book by Dr. Byron Lane will hold singular appeal. I commend it to you.

Reed M. Powell
President
International Symposium on
Small Business

Dr. Reed M. Powell has for many years been a member of the U.S. Small Business Administration National Advisory Council, which he has also served as Chairman. He is a member of the Advisory Committee for Small Business to the Secretary of the Treasury. He was instrumental in the formation of the Small Business Development Center Program. He has testified before Congressional committees and has consulted at high levels of government relative to the role of the small business and educational communities to the nation's economic welfare.

PREFACE

My work as a professor (a career change from that of an entrepreneur) in the School of Business and Management of a prominent West Coast university has brought me in contact with many hundreds of corporate and public-sector managers in mid-career. An astounding number of them are dissatisfied with their work and, as an inevitable corollary, with their whole lives.

The more they focus on their own personal growth, the more they become out of sync with corporate life. In their despair, they begin to flail away at the company's restrictive rules and policies and its ineptness at matching the nature of the job with the needs of human beings. When these managers and workers realize the futility of trying to change the monolithic corporate structure, they begin to look for a way out.

I have seen many of these women and men in "Career Changes" seminars and have been amazed that they overwhelmingly want out permanently—out of the controlling, life-denying hassle of a big organization. They want to do something on their own.

I began to contact others around the country in education and the helping professions. Everywhere my impressions were confirmed. The people of America are in the midst of a change in consciousness that is having its most dramatic impact on the nature of work.

While all this research was going on, I had started a book on small business, part of a promise to myself to make some of my experience and learnings available to practicing small business persons. I had assumed that my audience was the typical entrepreneur, born and raised with a passion to do his own thing, and having the classic risk-taking propensity. Certainly, many new ventures are started by these people, but the preponderance of today's new entrepreneurs fit few aspects of the classic model. They are bureaucratic escapees, seeking to fulfill themselves in a life-expanding, intrinsically rewarding small business of their own that will be part of their personal growth, as well as provide an income.

As the re-writes of the book began, I could see my focus changing. My life experiences as a successful small business person, my research and work with corporate people in mid-life crisis, and my new life as an educator were all combining to create an approach to small business ownership that is clearly different. It contains a view of the growing phenomenon of new-style entrepreneurs, some thoughts on self-fulfillment through small business ownership, and prescriptions for survival and success in a society that chews up new small business ventures at an alarming rate.

This book is not just about work—it is about the whole of life. There should be no separation between work and other life activities. The fulfilling life is all of a flow—there is no difference between work and play. Each person holds within himself the power to bring his life together if he chooses. If you are thinking about, or are already making this happen by doing your work *your* way, under your own control, then this book is for you.

I have used this material with young under-graduate students, mid-career managers, and corporate retirees who aren't ready to quit life. The one thing they all have in common is a zest for life, a real desire to fulfill their potential, and a need to continue the search for the meaning of their lives.

If this book touches you in any way, I will have re-enforced the meaning in my life. Thank you for allowing me to share with you.

Byron D. Lane

PART I

GETTING STARTED

The key to success in a business of your own is often in the initial phase. Correcting poor planning is much more painful than doing it right in the beginning. Even if your business is well under way, there are helpful ideas in the chapter "Starting A New Business."

The first chapter contains conceptual material important to the holistic aspects of small business ownership. It emphasizes that a business of your own must not only contribute to your economic well-being, it must be an integral part of your entire life-flow.

The chapter on transitioning is an area rarely considered in small business start-ups. It addresses ways to bridge the gap between a secure job and the risks of a new venture.

"Sources of Financing" contains some unusual ideas that will help you get started with less investment than you thought possible. For the continuing business, there are ways of freeing up capital for operating needs.

If you're considering a franchise, read about how to size up the human side of a franchiser as well as understanding his contractual obligations to you.

"Forms of Organization" suggests the best type for you and points out some real dangers in a partnership.

1. THE NEW ENTREPRENEUR

en-tre-pre-neur —"A person who organizes and manages any enterprise, esp. a business, usually with considerable initiative and risk."

Random House Dictionary of The English Language

Small business was once the exclusive habitat of the classic entrepreneur—the risk-taking, rugged individualist who started his own business primarily to make money. Recently, a new breed has entered the field; the primary motivation of this new breed is to get free. These women and men of all ages are part of a dramatic change in social consciousness. They are moved towards businesses of their own by two forces: (1) A growing dissatisfaction with the quality of worklife in large corporations and government bureaucracies. (2) A new ethic that places personal growth, self-fulfillment, and connectedness with the community of man above the acquisition of material things.

Not too long ago economic forecasters were predicting the demise of small business because of its inability to compete with the two hundred giant corporations that would soon dominate the nation's economy. New evidence suggests something quite different. Small business flourishes as big organizations continue to foster massive alienation through their inability to deal with the changing lives of workers.

Evidence of the changing order of things is all about us:

.. Surveys of people at work indicate that the new breed of workers stresses new values. One mentioned above all else is "being recognized as an individual person."[1] This is far different from the purely economic values of a few decades back.

1. Yankelovich, D. "The New Psychological Contracts at Work," *Psychology Today*, May, 1978, p. 49.

.. A recent Harris Poll showed that "basically, our people are far more concerned with the quality of life and far less with the unlimited acquisition of more physical goods and products." Those polled, by a substantial majority, said that:

—the country would be better off if children were educated more to find their inner satisfaction than to be a success and make a lot of money;

—economic growth falsely makes people want to acquire more possessions rather than to enjoy nonmaterial experiences;

—it is more important to learn to appreciate human values, as opposed to material values, than it is to find ways to create more jobs for producing more goods;

—they want more emphasis on breaking up big things and getting back to more humanized living rather than to develop bigger and more efficient ways of doing things.[2]

.. For the past three years, except for a rare few months, the top ten list of best selling books has included one or more on personal growth. The number of new issues in this category keeps increasing as publishers capitalize on the public's urge to find new meaning in life and a way to fulfill individual potential.

.. Voluntary simplicity is a rapidly accelerating lifestyle of the future. It is a way marked by a new balance between inner and outer growth. "It embraces frugality of consumption, a strong sense of environmental urgency, a desire to return to living and working environments which are of a more human scale, and an intention to realize our higher human potential—both psychological and spiritual—in community with others."[3] Figures indicate that already 15 million Americans embrace voluntary simplicity as a way of life, with another 60 million as sympathizers.

The people who embrace these visions know that their internal being must be matched to a compatible external environment and, in ever increasing numbers, they are leaving the large organizations to do something on their own.

CLASSIC VS. NEW ENTREPRENEUR

There is a clear distinction between the classic entrepreneur and the new entrepreneur. The model of the classic entrepreneur calls

2. *Congressional Clearing House of the Future.* "What's Next?", December, 1977 (Vol. 2, No. 6).
3. Elgin, **Duane S.**, and Mitchell, Arnold. "Voluntary Simplicity," *The Futurist,* August, 1977, p. 200.

up visions of pioneer businessmen whose rugged individualism and tenacity created the foundation for our present economy. Today's classic entrepreneur often has a visible heritage of business ownership. He, too, is a risk-taker and seeks a challenge. His primary motivation is a need for achievement and he uses money to keep score of his success. His focus is on units of production, the flow of goods, and other *things*.

The new entrepreneur may have some or all of the characteristics of the classic entrepreneur, but most often he fits few of the classic notions. His primary motivation is to get free by taking charge of his own life, to further his own personal growth, to improve his relationships, and to do his own work in his own way. He is just as likely to be successful as the classic entrepreneur, but he will probably limit the growth of his business rather than become an uncontrolled achiever. His primary focus is on people rather than things.

This does not mean that either group is wholly in one camp. There are a variety of strains of each. The one pervasive difference—the classic entrepreneur views people as a means to achieving bottom-line profitability, while the new entrepreneur sees bottom-line profitability as a portion of the process in enriching the quality of people's lives.

PROFILE OF THE NEW ENTREPRENEUR

Since each new entrepreneur first prides himself on his unique individuality, it would not do at all to create a series of neat little boxes that would be descriptive of the entire group. However, through hundreds of interviews, class discussions, and consultations, I have found that certain characteristics appear repeatedly. They can help us gain some measure of insight into this new person.

.. While the predominant age for starting a new venture remains in the thirties and forties, increasingly women and men at both ends of the age spectrum become business owners. It is not at all unusual to find successful businesses owned by enlightened people in their twenties. Similarly, as we begin to view aging in new ways, older people find second and third careers in a small business suited to their new self-concept.

.. In increasing numbers, the new entrepreneurs are women. Frustrated by lip service to equality while males dig in to preserve their dominance of large organizations, many competent women tire of punching clouds and move out on their own.

.. In early stages of the new entrepreneur's career, he worked in a large public or private bureaucracy. He was hooked by what seemed to be security and easy transferability within the organization and to other similar organizations. This notion exploded with wholesale layoffs during recent recessions. The passage of Proposition 13 in California, threatening or eliminating the most secure government positions, exacerbated his disenchantment.

.. The new entrepreneur sees the world about him as dynamic and himself as constantly evolving. He recognizes that the only enduring thing is change, and he does not want to be left at the post. This aspect of the new entrepreneur is particularly interesting. One of the characteristics attributed to the classic entrepreneur by writers and researchers is a moderate risk-taking propensity. What appears to be the same overt action on the part of the new entrepreneur comes about through his understanding of who he is, what his life is about, and a resultant deep belief in himself and his ability to survive, no matter what.

.. He cares deeply about the world around him, the ecology, and the connectedness of all living things.

.. He resists any dehumanizing process and is opposed to highly structured, inflexible bureaucratic institutions. His business exists for people, not the reverse.

.. He values education but finds most schools irrelevant. He seeks out those institutions that are innovative and meet his needs, rather than the needs of the institution.

.. He has a concern for congruence and simple honesty in his communication. He would rather not hide behind facades. In his organization, as in his life, he builds a climate of trust.

. . He believes he can create his life in his own way. He chooses to be free and not live by others' *oughts* or *shoulds*. He believes that the only limitations he has are those he puts on himself.

. . His business may be highly specialized, but he sees himself as a generalist and does not like being classified in any finite way. He enjoys diverse and creative projects.

. . He is in touch with himself and is willing to continually explore who he is and who he is becoming. For him the magic is not in the completion—it is in the process.

. . While he appreciates his cognitive capability, he acknowledges and values his feelings and those of others.

. . His secret weapon, that he uses with great effect on his big business competition, is his intuition. He keeps it finely tuned by listening to the messages of his own body and by increasing the holistic, non-linear capacity of his brain.

What was once a select group of people, viewing themselves and the world in exciting new ways, is now a dramatically growing force that may change the definition of success in small business from pure profitability to total fulfillment.

EVOLVEMENT STAGES OF THE NEW ENTREPRENEUR

In my research on the new entrepreneur I have been able to identify stages that most women and men go through in their evolvement towards self-employment.

Stage One—Wondering

Persons in this stage begin to feel dissatisfaction with one or more facets of their lives. Usually it begins with the job. They may have been passed over for advancement, had their creativity stifled, or find themselves simply bored. They may see little in their work future except a gold watch.

Instead of each day beginning with excitement, it begins with dread. Rather than enjoying each moment, they look forward to the end of the workday and fulfill themselves through hobbies or other activities.

This *dis-ease* with a substantial portion of daily life leads to a whole array of problems, often including the disintegration of a marriage or primary relationship. In advanced stages, physical signs of stress illness may appear. If the warning signs have been ignored until now, the body makes it perfectly clear that something needs to be done to alter a declining lifestyle. Symptoms may be varied such as a feeling of moving towards sickness rather than well-ness. Others get more severe signs, such as migraine headaches, or stomach and intestinal disorders. Those who continue to hold out against dealing with their real needs may even experience high blood pressure and heart disorders.

Many people spend the portion of their lives until retirement in Stage One. These are the great legions of the walking dead—human shells filled with despair, awaiting the time when they can stop working and begin to live. Unfortunately, retirement rarely changes anything.

Stage Two—Searching

The awakening persons embark on a very different journey. They recognize early the need to shift the direction of events and begin to search for ways to make this happen. Sometimes new awareness comes about through reading from the many books and articles on the subject of human potential. Contact with others in search of themselves may set off a spark. Many alive persons involve themselves in continuing education, and through the regenerative class-room processes they begin to examine ways to change. Whatever the start-up mechanism selected, recognition of the need for change is the catalytic factor.

Stage Three—Beginning

As the awakening process proceeds, the need for a new job, or quite likely an entire new career, becomes apparent. Persons in this stage seek help through career counseling, self-help groups or psychotherapy. This period is simultaneously painful and joyous as people actively begin to take control of their lives.

The search may take them through examination of how they came to their present occupation and what new occupation might suit the person they are becoming in the change process. It is in this stage that the possibility of getting free through a business of one's own is explored.

Stage Four—Realizing

The continuing search for identity leads to new and more satisfying stages of personal growth. As one finds inner peace and satisfaction, the disparity between this personal space and the external environment becomes increasingly irksome. Persons at this level have very little choice. In order to complete their journeys in a confluent manner they need to bring their lives into harmony. This can only be done by getting free of organizational life and beginning ventures of their own.

BUSINESSES STARTED BY NEW ENTREPRENEURS

Who are these new entrepreneurs, and where do we find them? Many are owners of the clothing boutiques, leather stores, pottery shops, plant stores, and other types of specialty stores that have changed the flavor of many large shopping malls and created new, interesting areas in our major urban centers.

Others have started small enterprises that offer specialized services to individuals, industry, and government. Light manufacturing and crafts ventures employ low technology and bring back highly valued handwork to a variety of items.

You can certainly see evidence of the new entrepreneurs in our universities. Courses in small business have become among the most popular in many schools of business. The new entrepreneurs are in ample evidence in my own classes. How often I hear, "I may go to work for a big business at first, but just to learn. I won't stay with them. They don't respect the environment." Or, "Big corporations are too impersonal. I need to be me, and I can express myself best in a business of my own."

Many of the new entrepreneurs are young and go into a venture fresh out of school. Others plod along in big organizations until one day they can stand it no more. One man I know in his forties has had a successful career with a major aerospace firm. Recently, he purchased a flower shop. His wife will run it, and he will help out on weekends. As soon as the shop goes well, he will leave his job and join the new venture full time. His reason; "I've been with this company for years, grinding my life away. They pay me well, but nothing happens that's exciting or gives me an opportunity to grow."

In one of my groups I worked with a woman of seventy, widowed and alone, sliding deeper and deeper into depression. Determined, she began a growth path that gave her new insights into how she could re-vitalize her life. Today, she runs a small thrift shop that supplies her need to be a part of the community and also serves as a life model for her friends and neighbors.

The businesses started by this new breed bear little resemblance to the entrepreneurial ventures of the past. At the heart of these entreprises is a concern for being free—free from an imposed hourly regimen; free from autocratic, bureaucratic dehumanization; free from the life-contracting boredom of non-creative work.

In addition to the traditional concern for economic viability, they ask questions such as these:

.. Does this business provide for full utilization of my creativity?
.. Does it augment my personal growth?
.. Does it provide a basis for enriching my human contacts?
.. Does it purvey meaningful goods or services as opposed to the mountains of junk that add to economic statistics rather than to the enhancement of life?
.. Does this business fit me and who I am?
.. Can I make decisions that keep the business flexible enough to grow and change with me?
.. Am I always in control, so that I can select only business that will be satisfying to me?
.. Can my family or those with whom I am in a primary relationship participate, so that the business will be a vehicle for our coming together, rather than a job I have to do that will keep us apart?

WHO SUCCEEDS?

Any number of books and articles on entrepreneurship and small business management purport to describe the person most likely to succeed. This occurs through careful listing of characteristics, even as I have done. The implication is that if you do not fit most of the categories, you should probably not go into business for yourself.

While I believe that this is well-intentioned advice, it is out of step with the changing national consciousness, and harmful to most entrepreneurs. Some clarifications are in order:

Myth: Sons-of-bitches succeed and nice guys fail in small business.

New age wisdom: All attempts at strategy are met by resistance and counter-strategy. Every aware person knows when he is being used. The successful entrepreneur uses things, never people. If you enjoy being a son-of-a-bitch, you will probably find more soul-mates in some of the larger institutions of our culture.

Myth: Aggressiveness is the essential characteristic of an entrepreneur.

New age wisdom: Super aggression is the outward manifestation of unresolved personal problems and often is the precursor to heart attacks and other stress disease. Many people start businesses of their own to get away from over-aggressive bosses.

Myth: The emotional need to win possesses the soul of the entrepreneur.

New age wisdom: The growing person has no need for recognition by beating anyone at anything. He only satisfies his own needs in harmony with those he loves. This doesn't mean that he can't be very successful, but *he* sets the standards of success.

Myth: Business owners are gregarious and extroverted.

New age wisdom: There is no one type of behavior that spells success, just as there is no such thing as a "sales type." Any behavior is effective if it works for you.

Myth: If you don't have the requisite characteristics to become an entrepreneur, you can't get them.

New age wisdom: Nothing in life is fixed. Any person can be who he wants to be. All it takes is the desire to grow and the willingness to risk.

Work is not a separate part of existence. It is an integral part of life. For life to be flowing and satisfying, work must be in harmony with all aspects of your being. The whole-person business also recognizes that making money is a critical part of the venture. Businesses operated on the brink of disaster are rarely a joy to anyone. Financial success is essential to survival of the business and to staying free. The trick is to have it all—a business that will provide fulfillment, meaning, and a satisfactory standard of living. The purpose of this book is to guide you in that total quest.

Additional Information

1. Samuel A. Culbert. *The Organization Trap, and How To Get Out Of It.* Basic Books, Inc., 1974. (Paperback) Describes how organization mantraps cause us to end up unhappy on the job.
2. Roy P. Fairfield, Editor, *Humanizing The Workplace.* Prometheus Books, 1974. A collection of articles about the dehumanization of the workplace and some possible solutions for worker alienation.
3. Louis F. Davis and Albert B. Cherns, Editors. *The Quality of Working Life.* The Free Press, 1975. Addresses the problems of creating a humane working environment.
4. Harold C. Lyon, Jr., *It's Me and I'm Here!* Delacorte Press, 1974. One sensitive human being's story of his transition from a West Point overachiever to a more fully functioning person. Illustrative of many of the mid-life career changes I see more frequently.
5. Gail Sheehy. *Passages.* Bantam Books, 1976. (Paperback) Everyone over thirty should read this.
6. Jack R. Gibb. *Trust: A New View of Personal and Organizational Development.* Guild of Tutors Press, 1978. (Paperback) This is the best book about the human condition on the contemporary scene. Everything you want to know about the "whole person" is right here.
7. E. F. Schumacher. *Small Is Beautiful: Economics As If People Mattered.* Harper and Row, 1975. (Paperback) This surprising book is must reading for anyone starting a business. It's nice to have an economist point to "small" as a better way for western life.

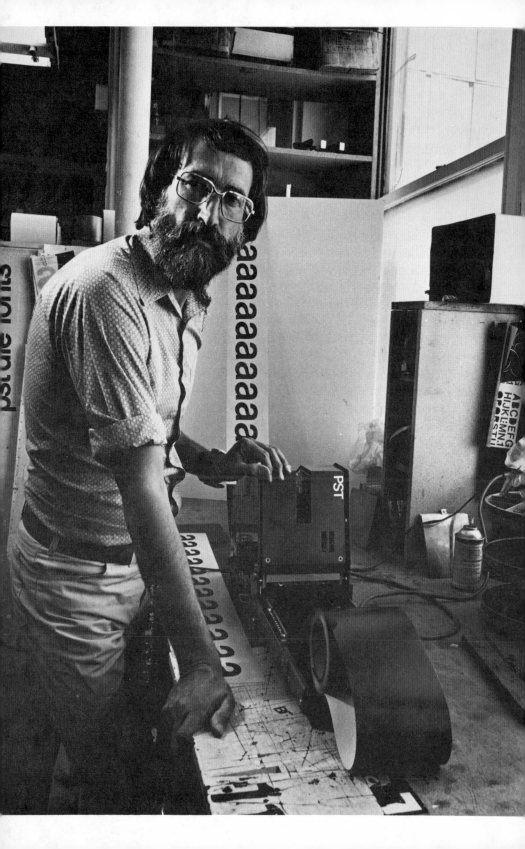

2. STARTING A NEW BUSINESS

Whenever statistics come out on business failure, the cause given most emphasis is "poor management." That type of generalized statement is not very helpful, so I am going to be very specific: In my experience, most of the problems that crop up in the first three years of a business' life (both economic and personal) can be avoided by careful planning.

Most small business ventures just happen—they are not planned. Having good taste in clothes or being a good cook is not enough to go into business today. No matter how much you want to "fly by the seat of your pants," resist the urge! Once the business is soundly started, then let all the creative part of you go and have fun. But, at the beginning, prepare a comprehensive and detailed Business Plan.

Often I have spoken to people with wonderful new business ideas. I *always* recommend that they do absolutely nothing until a complete Business Plan has been formulated. After weeks of research and writing, some discover that their idea just does not constitute a viable enterprise. This is valuable learning if it prevents another business failure.

There is no way to overestimate the importance of the Plan. To do it properly will require a minimum of several weeks work to as much as several months. The goal of your plan should be to make it so clear and so complete that you can put it on the desk of your friendly banker, walk away, and have him grant you a loan on the strength of the document alone.

Everyone who has completed the Business Plan under my direction counts it as one of the amazing and exciting experiences of his career. If you put the same zest into your Plan as into the running of your business, you will be rewarded with new insights and a feeling of real control over your destiny.

A sound Business Plan will serve many purposes:

1. It will lead you into seeing how your business fits into the marketplace.

2. It will uncover any flaws in your idea.

3. It will help you determine your marketing strategy.

4. It will give you accurate capital requirements. (Most start-up capital is arrived at by guesswork, and this often leads to under-capitalization.)

5. It will enable you to foresee the profit potential, which is of prime importance in your go/no-go decision.

6. It will provide a complete document for your banker or potential investors.

7. It will serve as a performance guide during your first few years of operation.

BUSINESS PLAN

  I. The Business Concept
    A. General statement of the purpose and objectives of the enterprise
    B. Definition of the market served
    C. Description of the products/services to be offered

  II. The Management Team
    A. Qualifications of key managers
      1. Capsulized resumes
      2. Description of functions to be performed
    B. Organization chart
    C. Ownership, stock distribution

  III. Products/Services Offered
    A. Detailed product/services description
    B. Proprietary features

C. Pricing
D. Customer benefits
E. Completeness of product line
F. Specialization emphasis
G. Quality and durability
H. Design and styling

IV. Marketing
   A. Market segmentation
   B. Growth trends
   C. Channels of distribution
   D. Sales strategy
   E. Promotion and advertising policy
   F. Competition
   G. Company image

V. Operations
   A. Lease/own facilities (including layout and design)
   B. Location
   C. Inventory and inventory control
   D. Equipment
   E. Quality control
   F. Make or job-out decision
   G. Raw materials/key vendors

VI. Financial Strategy
   A. Income statements and balance sheets (projected at least 3 years)
   B. Cash flow projections (at least 3 years)
   C. Capital investment
   D. Sources of capital

VII. Concluding Summary
   A. Growth scenario
   B. Risk analysis

VIII. Appendix
   A. Supplementary documents
      1. Leases
      2. Stories from trade papers

3. Supporting photographs or drawings
4. Research data
5. Patents and trade-marks
6. Logo identification

THE BUSINESS CONCEPT

The initial portion of your plan is an overview of your business idea. Many new ventures just begin with no idea of what they're about, and this is particularly true in retailing. How many times have you walked into a shop and out again wondering just what it was they were selling or trying to do? How many times did you get a clear message from a store? The clear message comes from careful planning, which naturally leads to *identification.*

Look at a number of really successful small ventures and chances are you will see something common to all of them. They "flow"— everything about the business seems to hang together. That's identification. It's the result of the owner/manager having an understanding of what it is he wants his business to be and to accomplish, and then carefully orchestrating each visual impression, each sound, each movement toward his goal. To begin creating your business concept, try developing answers to these questions:

1. What business am I in? (Not just the general category, but my area of specialization. See the part in Chapter 8 about the importance of specialization.)

2. What will make my business different from the competition? (Specifically, detail by detail.)

3. Who is my target customer?

4. Where is my market?

5. How do my life-style and this business fit together so that we "flow?"

6. Can I draw a picture (or could I tell an artist enough to enable him to draw it) of my business that would convey the whole story without words?

Look for answers in a variety of places. Examine similar operations. Identify the strengths that you can adopt. Identify the weaknesses to avoid. Talk to friends about your idea. Verbalizing will bring out more details. Someone may generate a thought you can develop. "Brainstorm" it!

Once you have the pieces, start to weave them together into a description of the business concept. Use whatever style comes naturally. One of the most effective ways is to describe a complete day in the life of the business. Conjure up a word picture of the business from opening to closing—the look of the building, the sign, the flow of material, the interaction of the personnel with the customers (some dialogue helps), how the business interacts with its environment.

Write, refine, and re-write until you have a complete concept that gives solid initial direction to your venture. The following is a straight narrative example for the concept portion of a business plan.

> *Apartment Living* is a retail home furnishings concept to fit the needs of a rapidly growing market. People who live in apartments, particularly those in high-rise urban types, lead a substantially different life-style than their home-owner counterparts. Their furnishings must fit six major criteria.
>
> 1. Wherever possible, items of furniture will fold, nest, or do double duty, e.g., dining tables will fold down, go into cabinets, or fold up the wall. Dining chairs, other than those used daily, will fold or stack. Occasional tables will nest or stack. Sofas will contain sleepers for guests or be the primary bed for one-room apartments. Case goods must stack or be wall-suspended.
>
> 2. All furniture pieces must be scaled to room size without sacrificing comfort.
>
> 3. Designs will be light, airy, and avoid a cluttered appearance to contribute to a feeling of spaciousness. This means chairs with pedestals will substitute for the four-legged variety wherever practical. Lamps will be of metal or wood, primarily, avoiding the large, shaded, heavy, ceramic type.
>
> 4. Designs will be modular in nature to fit the mobile life-style of apartment dwellers—they should adapt easily to a new environment. This puts an emphasis on sectional seating and modular wall systems.
>
> 5. The above criteria suggest that the only style able to fit all these needs is modern. This is compatible with the nature of the dwellings themselves and creates a harmonious atmosphere.

6. Functional accessories must fit into limited space. Dinnerware and glassware will be stackable. Cookware will consist of one unit cook-and-serve pieces.

The nature of the merchandise suggests that the primary sources of supply will be factories in Denmark, Norway, Sweden, and Italy. As American industry produces more specifically for these needs, domestic items will be introduced. Probably, a sizeable portion of the merchandise needs to be designed for the store. This suggests that a major role of *Apartment Living* will be as an industry trend-setter.

Substantial research (documented in the Appendix) suggests that the market segment for an *Apartment Living* store consists of relatively affluent business and professional men and women ranging in age from twenty-eight to forty. Another segment is retirees who have moved out of larger homes and need to refurnish because of smaller living space. The research shows that no matter what their previous furnishings style, a sizeable portion of older persons select modern design for their new life-style.

While most home furnishings stores need substantial display space, the design of an *Apartment Living* store is intended to demonstrate maximum utilization of living space, and will occupy considerably less display space than a traditional store. This means that the volume and profit per square foot will exceed industry standards, enabling utilization of a higher foot traffic location than is possible for a full-line furniture store.

The merchandising emphasis in *Apartment Living* is on the buying ability of the management rather than the selling ability of the personnel. The furnishings will be unique, relatively exclusive and displayed in ways that will either suggest their end use or dramatize their affordability. All displays will be accompanied by point-of-sales materials. This allows salespeople to be selected for their interior design ability rather than their high-pressure sales ability, again setting this store apart as a desirable place to shop.

Apartment Living will cover a broad middle price range, compatible with the dwellings and customers that will utilize its merchandise. While there is a substantial market at the lower price range, the design and quality of cheaper goods does not suggest itself for this concept. The upper price range is too limited for profitability if the concept is expanded into a multi-store chain.

Gross profit margins will be maximized through private labeling and selective purchasing. The limited selection, while adequate for the concept, will assure high turnover and low markdowns.

Apartment Living is a concept whose time has come. It caters to a market that has not yet been segmented by mass merchandisers or large chain furniture retailers. Its success will be largely based on selling a way of life rather than items of furnishings.

THE MANAGEMENT TEAM

As part of your Business Plan insert your own resumé. As you would on any planned job search, design the resumé to fit this particular situation. Highlight your experience, qualifications, and accomplishments that indicate you can be successful in this venture. This portion of the Plan will get a great deal of attention from loan officers.

If there are others in your organization who are owners, managers, or key employees, include information about them. Be concise, but don't leave out important details. If you are planning a stock company, describe present stock distribution, future plans, and options.

PRODUCTS/SERVICES OFFERED

This portion of your Plan should be a lively interpretation. You may need to use charts or drawings, but see if you can get into the presentation some of your enthusiasm for the product or service you will be selling.

If it is a retail business you are planning, examine the product mix (the line of merchandise) and how it will satisfy the wants and needs of your customer. For a service business, walk the reader through the complete process. A scenario format works well here. Manufacturers should detail every aspect of the product they will produce.

If you work this section well, you will find the very important marketing portion of your Plan will fall into perspective quite easily.

MARKETING

The first consideration here is: Who is my customer? Small enterprises rarely have a universal market, and it is most important to correctly identify the segment of the market that you are going to serve.

> In a recent seminar, one of the members was planning a business that would sell and install solar-powered heating units for homes. It created a lively discussion about who the target customers would be. While there are income tax allowances for purchase and installation of such units, the present state of the art indicates that it would be a minimum of ten years before the unit would pay for itself. With economic consideration not the primary selling feature, the market begins to narrow.
>
> The group decided that people with an immediate interest in solar power would probably have an interest in the conservation of natural resources. They then decided that such persons in the population would most likely have these characteristics: at least some college education, in the middle to upper middle income bracket, and in their thirties or early forties.
>
> Certainly solar-powered units have a much larger ultimate potential, but for a new business just beginning it seemed wise to focus on the population most likely to purchase these units.
>
> How to find such people? Study of the United States census tracts, readily available to everyone, would define the specific areas of a city where these persons predominate. The marketing device might then be a mailer designed to turn up live prospects.
>
> There are a lot more scientific and complete ways to determine a market for a product, but this example is illustrative of the initial thought processes that are necessary to bring a product and its potential market into focus.

Once you have a handle on who your customer is, have a look at where he is and how you're going to reach him. Plan your initial advertising and sales strategy and start to develop a budget to go with the action plan. You'll find yourself involved with the business image now, as it goes along with advertising.

Finally, take a hard look at the competition and make a complete statement on how your business will meet it. This is fundamental to your Plan and success. A careful study of others in your field will give you ideas of their weaknesses and strengths, which in turn will help to set the style of your business.

Don't short-cut this work. It will be surprisingly revealing. And don't limit yourself to the activities of the business—study the characteristics of the owner. If you can unearth the flaws in your competition, you may discover the niche for you.

OPERATIONS

This section is a description of the physical operation of the business. It is the place for you to document your decision whether to lease facilities and equipment or to buy them, how you will purchase and control inventory, and who will be your main suppliers.

For small manufacturing firms, the crucial decision about actually engaging in the production process or deciding to contract the work out is completely discussed.

FINANCIAL STRATEGY

It all comes together right here, when you make up your first profit projection. The expense details can be forecast with a great deal of accuracy—it is the sales figures that often become a juggling act. ⌐ on't fool yourself! Use your market research information and marketing plan to make *realistic* income assumptions. I have seen many Plans, months in the working, come down to the bottom line of the income projection only to find out that the business can never make a profit, or that the return on time and investment would be too small to be a viable venture.

It is my contention that if every new business proposal started out with a Business Plan, such as we have been illustrating, the national failure rate would go down considerably because there would be fewer marginal start-ups. So, if you find out in this way that your idea will not go, you can take satisfaction in the time, money and heartbreak you have saved—and, if you really want to get free in your own business, you will go back to the drawing board with an improved version or a new concept.

More hopefully, you will come up with figures that are exciting, not only to you but to potential investors. Next step: Do a cash flow analysis. If you are like most people I've worked with, you will find this an amazing experience. Once you see that there is often a wide discrepancy between your profit statement and your checkbook, you will never operate your business without regular cash flow forecasts. (Chapter 12, "Cash Flow" will be helpful.)

With all the profit and cash forecasts complete, you are ready to compute your capital requirements. When you are finished, if you require a loan, you will need to go back and re-do the profit and cash flow projection to include interest and principal repayments. In other words, this is a do-and-re-do job, until all the pieces fit, and you have triple-checked your work for accuracy.

Most entrepreneurs duck the financial planning. Don't you do it! Even if you work with your accountant, be sure you understand what's going on. You will be using this portion of the Plan later as an important tool in your business management.

CONCLUDING SUMMARY

The only attention usually given the growth scenario is when there is a serious attempt to attract investors. What they want to see is a substantial return on their investment. For the new entrepreneur, there may be another very important reason to have a look into the future. If you don't plan now, you may find yourself in uncontrolled growth. That situation has two sides: If you wish to have your business grow, you don't want it to grow broke. That happens often. Many good businesses grow out of cash and disappear through lack of planned financing. The other side is that many new-age small business persons don't want to grow. They just want to have a nice, comfortable income and run their own lives—not have the business run their lives. This also takes planning.

Lorraine G. and I were talking about plans for a mini-business of her own. She had been doing distinctive embroidery that was much in demand by members of the TORI community and had some real success with designing clothes that were simple and comfortable. Her idea was to create a short line of clothes that could be produced by hand and sold to specialty stores direct or through a California firm's label.

The merchandise she wanted to produce is in demand by an increasing number of people who are leading the way in open, casual life-styles. As we began to put the Business Plan together, it became evident that the sales curve was going to go up dramatically—which was exactly what she did not want. Her whole reason for the business was to create a small income, enjoy the creativity, and do it all in the context of her life, over which she has such beautiful control.

So, the planning needed to include such things as limited editions and a way to say no to large orders, without losing the customer forever.

This is business on another scale—not just how much money it can make, but how it can contribute to personal fulfillment.

Finally, put your completed Business Plan into a neat, typewritten package and bind it in a suitable way. Like every other part of your business, this document projects your image. How well you prepare it may make the difference between go and no-go in your new business venture.

GETTING FREE WITH LITTLE OR NO INVESTMENT

Thousands of new businesses start each year with a minimal investment, many with no money at all. The trick is in finding an opportunity, being creative, and, if necessary, using someone else's money. An idea for a new venture can be fresh and inventive, or it can be a rework of someone else's concept. Countless thousands of new ideas never get going because the originator gave up, couldn't see the potential, or was not able to do a real marketing job.

The first step is to get an idea for a product or service that you can handle by yourself or with members of your family.

.. Try the patent section of the public library. After seventeen years all patents enter the public domain. You may find an idea that can be re-vitalized or re-marketed in a new context.

.. Read through trade magazines in your area of interest. You may find a product or line that you can distribute.

.. Your own company probably has hundreds of unused ideas. Many are good but represent too small a market for a huge corporation. There could be an idea just the right size for you, and it could be in your own area of know-how.

.. Doctoral dissertations are usually thoroughly researched and future-oriented. Ask your local research librarian to help you use one of the retrieval systems. You may even be able to get into a team business with the writer.

.. Inventors shows offer a fantastic array of new products. Try your local United States Department of Commerce field office for a guide to events in your area.

.. Trade shows are great stimulators. Pick one in an area that interests you and just hang around talking to people.

.. Read the Business Opportunities section of the Sunday newspaper. Dozens of ideas will pop up. If you're really serious, subscribe to the Sunday *New York Times*. The number of ideas you'll find will be almost overwhelming.

.. Talk to salesmen operating in your industry. They know what the market needs.

.. Connect with venture capitalists and bankers. Often they have ideas and capital and are looking for an entrepreneur to develop them.

Here are some other thoughts on low capital ventures:

.. Be a consultant in your area of expertise. Start by creating attractive stationery and calling cards. Make some contacts and get referrals. You may just land a consulting contract. If not, you may get a dream job offer. Or, you may just fall over the product that will work for you.

.. Service business is the fastest growing part of the American economy. Learn to recognize needed services, then fill the need.

Warren B. was a senior project manager in aerospace. One day, thoroughly disenchanted, he walked out. For some time, he attempted to do a career switch into a new job. When he realized that he was going to get back into an 8 to 5, he started looking at what he could do on his own. One day, watching a plumber do some work at $30 per hour, he realized he could do the same work at far less. He let it be known around the area that he would do plumbing and simple maintenance at reasonable prices. Within weeks he was offered the maintenance contract for several apartment buildings.

He then ran an ad for women to train as maintenance workers and was flooded with replies. He selected several and set up a school training the women to do simple plumbing, painting, tiling, and repairs. The women were delighted. They could work part time, get out of the house, and make better wages than on typical women's jobs. Warren had an ample labor supply. The customers had workers who cared and at a reasonable price. This flourishing venture fills a need in the community and is the means for Warren's getting free forever.

. . Be an in-betweener. All you need to get started is stationery. Find a product from a foreign country. (There are hundreds of international trade magazines offering products.) Get the exclusive right to market it in the United States. Then go out and sell it! Billing is done by the manufacturer directly to the retailer, and you collect your commission. Add a few more products, and you have a going business.

Remember that the idea you're searching for requires little money, comes with money, or is so hot someone will provide the money. If you make a real search, you may turn up your way to get free.

Additional Information

1. Donald Dible. *Up Your Own Organization.* The Entrepreneur Press, 1974. (Paperback) This is must reading for anyone contemplating a new venture.
2. Gordon B. Baty. *Entrepreneurship: Playing to Win.* Reston

Publishing Company, 1974. Focus is on the problems of growth-oriented enterprises, as opposed to traditional small business. Important book if you're headed in that direction.

3. Joseph Mancuso. *Fun and Guts: The Entrepreneur's Philosophy.* Addison-Wesley Publishing Company, 1973. Mancuso is a practitioner and a teacher. This is a fun book, but read it for wisdom.

4. William D. Putt, Editor. *How To Start Your Own Business.* The MIT Press, 1974. Written by M.I.T. alumni who have started firms with high technology. Strictly for engineering types.

5. Louis L. Allen. *Starting And Succeeding In Your Own Small Business.* Grosset and Dunlap, 1968. There are many gaps in this book, but the author has been there and has things of importance to say. "How To Raise Money" chapter is good.

6. Gilbert Dorland and John Van Der Wal. *From Idea to Maturity.* Capital Services, 1976. For the growth-oriented firm, a very high-powered book on financing.

7. William David. *Not Quite Ready To Retire.* The Macmillan Company, 1970. For older men and women. First part is on jobs, but last third of book has many possibilities for turning hobbies or existing skills into a small business venture.

8. International Entrepreneur's Association, 631 Wilshire Boulevard, Santa Monica, California 90401 publishes booklets on eighty different businesses. Write for their catalogue.

9. Small Business Reporter, Bank of America, Department 3120, P. O. Box 37000, San Francisco, California 94137. Bank of America publishes a whole series of booklets on business operations and profiles of specific businesses. At $1.00 each, they're the best buy I know. Write for a list of titles.

10. Jeffry A. Timmons et al. *New Venture Creation.* Richard D. Irwin, Inc., 1977. Basically a university text, but it has a number of involvement exercises that can be useful in formulating a business plan.

11. Joseph R. Mancuso. *How To Start, Finance and Manage Your Own Small Business.* Prentice-Hall, 1978. (Paperback) A truly complete book by a real pro.

12. Jeffrey Feinman. *100 Surefire Businesses You Can Start With Little Or No Investment.* Playboy Press, 1977. There are 100 ideas listed. You decide if they are surefire.

3. MAKING THE TRANSITION TO YOUR OWN BUSINESS

Many prospective new business owners never get started because they are locked into the illusory security of a corporate job. I say "illusory" because business giants are also subject to the vagaries of the economy and, occasionally, to poor management. Wholesale layoffs of twenty-year management veterans are far from unknown in the corporate world.

In any case, jobs seem secure and most corporate families conduct their lives around regular paychecks. I have watched many women and men go through all the phases of starting a venture of their own, only to give up at the last moment because they were unwilling to take what they saw as "too big a risk."

The problem is that many people who hold positions in large public and private sector bureaucracies, and who have considered a venture of their own, have a mental picture that goes something like this:

Here I am in this warm, cuddling place where machines crank out paychecks that take care of me. All I need do is behave myself and I will make it to the gold watch. Except nothing is happening with my life. I am plodding away at an 8 to 5, living my real life at other hours.

Somewhere in my fantasy is a business of my own, where I can set my own pace, create my life my way, have the excitement and challenge that I want. But between here and there is a yawning chasm. The only way I can get there is to let go and take a big leap.

Fortunately, there are other scenarios. It is possible to build bridges—to make a transition to the new life, retaining the financial advantages of the old. In some ways bridging the gap is more difficult (and dangerous) than jumping. It requires double duty that can take a heavy toll on individuals and on families. But, if there is a genuine family joining in the process, the getting there can be the most growth-producing part of the entire adventure.

John W. was a student in my Human Resources Management class. He is a second-line manager with a large utility company, earning $25,000 a year. He is thirty-five years old, has three children ranging in age from four to ten. He has understood for some time that the company has provided him with an enormous security blanket to compensate for the lack of stimulation and advancement possibilities provided by the job.

In this course each student is encouraged to focus on himself and his own personal growth as the most important step in becoming a better manager of people. This is the first time John has taken a deep look at who he is and where he is going with his life. At one level he really knows that his life is unfulfilled and that he is trading off happiness for security, but because of what he sees as the best thing for his family, he avoids being in touch with himself and his needs.

As part of the group process, John and his classmates are learning to be personal, open, and sharing with each other. As John begins to get in touch with himself, some of his hidden feelings emerge. One day, in a career planning discussion, John is asked to take a fantasy trip five years into the future and describe a day in his life as he would want it to be. To no one's surprise, the idea that has been floating around in the back of his mind about going into his own business comes rushing out. He describes himself in his office in a small plant he owns. His business is manufacturing and marketing several of his own inventions.

It turns out that the inventions are actually in prototype stage now. His hobby is tinkering with new consumer items, and he spends his spare time at the bench in his garage workshop. But none of these very fine items has ever been brought

to production model stage, and he has not applied for patents. As the group interaction proceeds, he says that he is afraid of the next step. If he really makes his inventions viable products for marketing, he will have to go ahead and start his business. What will happen if it fails? How will he take care of his family's needs during the formative years of the business? What about his pension plan? John is now in a psychological double bind—damned if he does, damned if he doesn't.

For John there are alternatives to "start" or "don't start." He can consider a transition period, starting the new venture gradually while holding on to the secure job. There are several ways he can approach this:

1. One possibility is for John to bring his inventions to a final stage and apply for patents. He can then look for a manufacturer already marketing items of a similar nature as a potential buyer for his product. If it is a viable item, he may be able to get an amount of cash plus royalties over the life of the product. He can do the same with the other items and then go on to new inventions. His first decision will revolve around his own desires. Does he primarily want to be an inventor, or does he want to be a business administrator? This is a clear fork in the road and needs a decision. Serious inventors sometimes make poor business administrators.

2. If owning the business is John's choice, there are also ways to make the transition. He can find a manufacturing company with excess capacity to produce the product to John's specifications. In this case, he will have minimum investment and no production responsibilities. The manufacturer may even pack and ship. Next, he can retain a marketing organization to take over distribution. A few organizations are national. More likely, he will need to retain manufacturers' representatives area by area. These groups work strictly on commission and get exclusive areas to cover. The best way for John to contact them is at trade shows.

With the manufacturing, shipping, and marketing set, the balance of the job is promotion and paperwork. It is possible to do this, utilizing the family or a few skilled employees who can work under minimum supervision. When sales and profits increase to the desired level, John quits his job. He has made the transition.

3. What's that, John? You say you want to go right into a small

plant of your own and do assembling, contracting out only components? And you want to keep your job, too? That's a tall order, John, but here's a way: Find some bright young person who is really capable of handling the plant's operations. Make a deal where he gets a piece of the business. Work the new business part time while drawing your pay on the job. When the business grows, and you move in full time, your partner can run an enlarged plant while you concentrate on sales.

Barbara C. is a psychiatric social worker, working primarily with juveniles. She is a warm, caring person, and her performance record is excellent. In the process of growing and searching for the meaning of her life, she finds herself increasingly at odds with the bureaucratic system that perpetuates incompetency, rewards longevity, and pays less and less attention to the plight of the client or the source of the problem.

She, too, retains a need for the pervasive security of the system's cradle-to-grave benefits and regular paychecks as she reaches for control over her own life.

The struggle manifests itself in a variety of physical symptoms—excessive weight gain, stiffness in the neck, elevated blood pressure. As a professional, Barbara has a thorough understanding of the relationship between her emotional struggle and physical illness. She sets about systematically working the problem through a holistic health program. One day in a Career Changes group, she realizes that the ultimate answer is in creating her own environment—in getting free through a business of her own.

Barbara's skills and knowledge naturally lead her to exploring a consulting career, but the problem of making her transition is still there. She begins by assessing her strengths and matching them against the needs in the community. She then seeks out speaking engagements wherever prospective clients gather. Some of this is done in connection with her regular job, some in off-time through her professional associations. In the early stages of her program she has been offered several consulting opportunities. What is different now about Barbara is that she sees herself moving towards independence. This generates an aliveness in her that increases her speaking and interpersonal effectiveness, which increases her confidence, which improves her health, which drives her further toward increasing her potential. Barbara's time is going to be full handling two careers, but eventually she will generate enough income in her own business to let go of the job.

Marcy and Don, who share their bee supply venture with us in a later chapter, are another example of transitioning. As a two-income family, their resolution of how to get free is to risk one income only, Marcy's, while the new business is building. She runs the daily affairs of the business; he handles the books and works weekends. When the business is returning enough to support them both, he will leave his job and join the new venture.

There are countless other ways to transition into a business of your own. Many successes began on the kitchen table. Try taking your idea and reducing it to units of work that can be done on weekends. Then, before you make your move, let the business grow until it can only be handled on a full-time basis.

Ideally, a business should be started with a full investment of your time and energy, but if the risk looks too great consider building bridges. The important thing is to get started. The energy generated by making the decision will have a salutary effect on all the activities of your life.

Additional Information

This is a new concept without prior references. You might contact your SCORE representative at the nearest Small Business Administration office and ask him to refer you to people who have made transitions. It's going to be a bit of trouble, but the least that can happen is that you will get moral support in your effort.

4. BUYING AN EXISTING BUSINESS

There are many self-proclaimed experts in the field of buying and selling a business. Unfortunately, after you listen to all the advice and do all the necessary evaluating, you will find yourself totally alone in the final decision-making process. The real worth of a business is how much it's worth to you, and there are no acceptable, simple formulas. There are some very important guidelines to help you along the way and, just as you would in a new start-up of your own, use all the information you can gather, check each aspect of the business thoroughly, get all the advice possible.

ADVANTAGES AND DISADVANTAGES OF BUYING A GOING BUSINESS

Some advantages:

.. Attractive terms may be available. If the assets have been depreciated, you may find purchase cheaper than starting a new venture. You might even find an older owner who will sell for a payout based on future profits.

.. The business may have contracts, patents, leases, that you cannot obtain for a new start-up.

.. This is a going concern. Hopefully, it has customers and orders. It may have an organization that will continue through a change of ownership.

.. New ventures are highly speculative, but an ongoing one has a track record that can be evaluated both as to history and as an aid to plans for the future.

.. A going business is a single-purchase transaction as opposed to the myriad of purchases needed for a new venture.

.. If the business has a good record, financing may be easier to obtain.

.. Less planning is needed.

.. Profits come sooner.

Some disadvantages:
.. The business may have a number of problems, and you will inherit them.

.. The business may be successful but carry lines of merchandise that don't fit your taste or style. There is a danger in re-merchandising.

.. The terms may be unattractive.

.. The physical assets may need modernization.

.. The business may have a well-established image that does not fit your personality.

.. The capital investment probably will be larger than that required if you are starting your own business.

.. Walking into a full-blown business is unlike growing with one. You will need to learn fast and under pressure.

HOW TO FIND A BUSINESS TO PURCHASE
.. Local newspapers and *The Wall Street Journal* carry listings in the classified section under "Business Opportunities."

.. Business brokers handle sales on a commission. Watch out here. There are many honest brokers, but remember they are interested in the sale, not in you.

.. Trade papers handle ads of businesses for sale. This is the best place to start if you are looking for a venture in a specific industry.

.. Business associations will know of sale possibilities.

.. Accountants and lawyers are the first to hear when a client wants out. If you are interested in a specific geographical area, try letters to these professionals.

EVALUATING A BUSINESS FOR SALE

Whatever is covered here will *not* be comprehensive. Read everything you can on this subject. Then do your evaluation. Before you make a decision, consult experts—people who have been through it, accountants who specialize in this type of work, a few SCORE members at the Small Business Administration, and finally an attorney.

These are a few ideas for starters:

.. Check carefully into the real reason for selling. Many offerings are in bad shape or the market conditions are changing, but the cover statement may be, "for reasons of health."

.. Get the financial statements for several years. Start with the current balance sheet. Does it reflect a sound condition? Now, go deeper to see if the figures are realistic. Examine the inventory to determine if it is accurately valued, then the accounts receivable ledger to see if payments are current. This job requires painstaking attention to detail.

.. Check income statements for several years. What is the profit trend? What are the real earnings? (E.g., are they unrealistic as a result of skimming cash and charging borderline personal items, or are they overstated as a result of inflating sales or undervaluing purchases?)

.. What is the pricing formula of the firm? Is it current with competition, or will it need re-thinking?

.. How about the fixed assets? What is their real value to you? Are they modern and in good condition?

.. What is the position of the firm in regard to its competition?

.. What is the current size and the future of the market?

.. How effective are the personnel? What is the effectiveness of the management team?

.. How do others in the industry regard the character of the seller and the business itself?

.. If there are leases expiring or that need transferring, check to see what the terms will be in a transfer to you, or if you will need to negotiate a completely new arrangement.

.. What is the future of this industry?

You can probably add a number of items to this list. The idea is clear—no amount of analysis is too much.

HOW MUCH TO PAY?

This question is unanswerable in any definitive way. It's what the business is worth to you, and there is a difference in the eye of each beholder. There are some starting points, however. One method is to evaluate the assets on their market worth (not necessarily book value), and then negotiate from there.

If a business is successful, chances are the price is going to be based on a multiple of earnings and the range will be between three and fifteen times after-tax income. Try looking at the transaction this way: The assets represent an amount you can put a real value on, and whatever else you pay is risk. The amount of return on investment you want and estimate you can get versus the quality of the risk will determine the range in which you will negotiate.

An interesting aspect now comes up—very often it is the terms of payment that become more important than the price you will pay. For example, if you can purchase a successful going business for a small amount of cash and extended payments, even though the total price is high, it might be advisable to do so since you will be paying for the business out of earnings. It might also allow you to get into your own business with an amount of cash too small for a start-up. Complex factors are involved such as taxation and leverage, and you are well advised to get competent assistance in your evaluation of how much to pay and the method of payment.

MAKING THE DECISION

One of the great dangers in purchasing a business is falling in love with it to the point where you get blinded by its beauty. I certainly hope that you will be truly smitten with the venture you enter and that it will lead to a life of fulfillment where work and play all become one. Unfortunately, in the business world love does not conquer all. Check the business out just as dispassionately as you would a used car. Then, after you own it, start your love affair.

I have been on the selling end of the franchise business, and I have seen numerous totally irrational decisions made involving tens of thousands of dollars. Fortunately, for my own peace of mind, the opportunity I sold really did live up to its promise. I have also witnessed families' life savings wiped out because they didn't check out other offerings. If you start a new business, you will do thorough preparation. Don't do any less for purchase of an existing one.

As a final method, to make sure you cover all the bases in your evaluation of a business, try a turn-around. Imagine you are the owner of the business and you plan to sell it. What steps might you take to inflate the earnings, even knowing you would up your taxes? You might value the inventory a bit higher. You might stop charging off questionable items, etc. Be wise—investigate!

Additional Information

1. *How To Buy and Sell a Small Business.* Drake Publishing, 1975. Mini-book provides good basic coverage.
2. Bank of America. *How To Buy Or Sell A Small Business.* Vol. 8, No. 11, 1973. Available at a Bank of America branch or send

$1.00 to Small Business Reporter, Bank of America, Department 3120, P. O. Box 37000, San Francisco, California, 94137.
3. The SBA has regional seminars on this subject. Call the local office for information.
4. Kenneth J. Albert. *How To Pick The Right Small Business Opportunity.* McGraw-Hill, 1977. Chapter 12, "Selecting An Ongoing Business," provides simple but comprehensive guidelines.

5. SOURCES OF FINANCING

The ultimate frustrations: (1) You have been developing the idea for a new business venture for over a year. Your research is thorough, you have bounced the concept off some prominent experts in the field and have put together a superb business plan. You begin to approach investors and bankers. Most conversations go like this: "A great idea. You have worked out the details nicely. You seem to be just the person who can make it all happen, but—." The big word is "but." It doesn't matter what was said first—everything starts at "but." The rest of the message sounds like a stale marriage. "It's too hot, it's too cold. It's too late. We are over-invested. We don't have the funds. It's the wrong time of the year. It's the wrong century."

(2) You are in your third year of business. Things are going extremely well—in fact, too well. Your sales are running way ahead of projection. Your profits are excellent. And, you are running out of cash. You gather up your financial statements with all your projections and in high good humor pay a visit to your friendly banker. He knows you well. You have been doing business with him since you started. He looks over all the material and says, "You must be pleased with your progress. Your business is certainly looking good, but—."

This is the reality of life for most small ventures. Start-ups must rely heavily on the entrepreneur's own resources: savings, equity in his home, life insurance cash value. Expansion comes the hard way, from retained earnings. Though big business has the advantage of access to public funds and extensive lines of credit, there *are* ways for the inventive small business person to acquire or conserve capital. Let's start with the more obvious ones and then go into the more unusual and lesser known.

EQUITY CAPITAL

This is hard way number one. It's your idea, your planning, and your work. You do not have the necessary capital, so you take in Mr. Moneybags as a permanent, silent partner. More than likely, it's someone you know in the community, a friend, or a relative. He just puts up a hunk of the money, sits back, and waits for you to make it multiply. To your advantage, equity capital is money you don't have to pay back. Many small businesses just don't have the potential to support the owner and make huge debt payments, so taking in a partner is the only way. The figures you develop in your business plan will probably influence your choice of equity versus debt funding.

Most writers and practitioners are quite firm in their statements not to get involved with family as either silent or active partners. I have had both good and bad experiences with relatives. It really is a risky affair at best. Unless your relationship is built on mutual trust and open communication, don't work with members of your family as partners.

I have recently arrived at an arm's-length solution that works for me. If I enter a business deal I really believe in, I will seek capital from friends and family. However, I don't take money based on love —a strict business deal is formulated. I commit everything to detailed writing. There are legal notes to cover most contingencies. If there is a corporation involved, I personally guarantee any notes. I also take out insurance on my life to cover the amount of notes or any buyout considerations. Finally, I pay interest and/or provide equity commensurate with the risk. I like to see the deal constructed in such a way that an outsider can agree it is a sound arrangement for all parties. If you do this, I believe you can take advantage of a readily available source of funds and still feel comfortable with the transaction.

A final word on equity. If you have not yet decided on the business you will begin, think about buying a going business and paying for it out of profit. There are many such deals to be had, particularly where there is an older person or couple involved. If you really hunt, you may be able to get on-the-job training plus a whole business, with no money down. It's worth investigating.

DEBT FUNDING

If your capital needs can be handled by a loan, by all means do it this way before selling equity in your business. You will need to have a very good business plan and confidence in your ability to make it work.

It is certainly better to pull in your belt for several years and then own the whole business than to share with a partner, particularly one who is not active. You will face a few hard years, but the independence is more than worth it.

Commercial Banks

The obvious starting place for a loan is at a commercial bank. If you need short term money (less than a year) for inventory buildup, to take advantage of special buys, or other temporary cash needs, you can go this unsecured way. If you have been in business for a while, are regularly making a profit, can document how the money will be used, and if the amount is reasonable (well, these restrictions are not *too* bad), you are quite certain to score.

Many entrepreneurs I know take out these types of loans regularly, often when they don't really need them. The purpose is to build a line of credit and to have a record of prompt payment.

When I was in my first business for just six months, I applied for and received a 90-day inventory loan of $1,500. The next year, I asked for $2,500 and got it. By the fourth year, I could get $6,000 for up to six months with just a phone call to the bank. A few years later, I sold out and moved to another state. When I wanted to open a new business, I went to a local bank and, based on my prior record of payment, asked for and received a three-year unsecured term loan of $25,000. This figure continued to escalate. I have known entrepreneurs with open lines of credit in the high six figure amounts.

Admittedly, this is a tedious route to avoid the "buts." Yet, it is one of the best avenues of quick money for small business persons.

Pete M. was an enterprising university student who lived in a recreation vehicle with bunk-style beds. One day he became particularly irritated at having to use flat bed sheets because there was no fitted variety available for his odd-sized bed. With the assistance of his girlfriend and her sewing machine, he made several flat sheets into fitted ones.

The idea came to him that there might be a substantial market for fitted sheets for recreational vehicles. So, he sewed up some to fit a range of bunks, packaged them in plastic containers (along with re-order information), and made some contacts with distributors at a recreational vehicle show.

Orders began to trickle in, so he found a loft, bought a used sewing machine, and gathered some of his friends. They began to convert flat sheets they purchased at retail into recreational vehicle fitted ones. The profit was pretty good and the deposits with the orders assured his continuing without any capital investment. The business provided beer money until he got the big idea.

Pete called on a major vehicle manufacturer and suggested that he supply each new vehicle with a set of fitted sheets for each bunk. He would package and supply the sheets. (Of course, with a direct re-order card inside. What does a person do with one set of sheets?) This little effort resulted in a $35,000 order, which would produce $12,000 profit to Pete.

Now he needed to buy material direct from the mill, get a slightly better machine, and buy packaging in quantity. With no line of credit, the mill wanted money in advance. Help!

Pete now developed a complete Business Plan. With his plan and a bona fide purchase order for $35,000 from a AAA-1 manufacturer, he went to the bank. Without one cent of his own, he obtained a loan for $15,000.

Banks are a good starting place for term loans of one to five years, but if yours is a new business, this is another hard way. You may qualify if you already have 50% of your capital needs, have a solid record of success in the type of business you are entering, and if you have a business plan that is convincing. More than likely, you will still need collateral or the guarantee signature of your millionaire uncle.

Expansion capital for a going business with a solid track record is a bit easier to secure, providing it is not too hot, or too cold, or too. . . . Don't give up hope, read on. There *is* a way to get money from banks.

SBA Loans

Most entrepreneurs believe that Small Business Administration loans are difficult to get. That is quite true of direct loans, for which only a limited amount of money is appropriated by Congress. But there's another type of SBA loan, the bank guarantee, that is readily available. It works this way: You go through a presentation to a bank of your choice and get turned down for a loan. You go to a second bank and are refused. Perhaps on to a third refusal. Now, you decide which of these banks you would like to work with and ask if they will go along with an SBA guaranteed loan. Chances are good they will agree, since they will have the guarantee of the United States Government.

Now, you go to the local SBA office and present your plan. If they believe your plan is sound, and if you have at least 30% to 40% of your own money in the deal, and if they decide the three banks turned you down because it was too hot or too cold, they will start the process of the loan guarantee.

One word of caution here. The SBA does not want losers either. Be sure you are prepared with a complete plan covering every detail. There are fee agents who help prepare SBA proposals. You don't need them for most purposes, and the SBA doesn't like to see you spending money on proposals that could go into the business. You will find the folks at SBA helpful. The only reason for the existence of this agency of the United States Government is to assist small business persons.

Now, use all the patience at your command. Working with the SBA is a long, drawn-out process with mountains of paperwork. SBA administrators keep talking about getting loans processed in three days. I would plan on more like three weeks or three months. What's important is that you *can* get this guarantee (the SBA guarantees 90% of your loan at the bank) quite readily because there is no limit on the amount the SBA can guarantee. Too few people take advantage of this really terrific program for small entrepreneurs. If you get an SBA guaranteed loan, you have additional advantages in the form of free management assistance. See the chapter, "Where To Get Help" for important information about these services.

Commercial Finance Companies

You may want to buy out a partner, acquire another business, or get into a situation that even the SBA won't accept. Commercial finance companies charge some heavy interest rates, but they may solve your problems. They also will buy accounts receivable, releasing substantial sums of money for other purposes.

Credit Unions
For quick cash, there's no place like your own credit union. They can loan up to $2,500 unsecured and $10,000 with security.

LITTLE KNOWN SOURCES OF CAPITAL
There are many more sources of investment capital, most for larger sums of money. If you're interested in big money, try some of the books at the end of this chapter. Most small business persons are looking for amounts of money that don't interest the big boys. So, here are some more esoteric ways of getting and keeping capital. Most of them don't interest the big boys either, but they may make all the difference to you.

Trade Suppliers
Some trade suppliers are interested in helping a new account if they feel it may turn into a substantial one in the future. This help may take the form of extended credit terms, even loan guarantees. It is not unheard of for some suppliers to actually put people in business. Make bold inquiries. The downside risk is only a rejection.

Equipment Manufacturers
Consider leasing equipment. This conserves the down-payment you would make on installment financing. Leasing may be more expensive in the long haul, but it just may get you into business or free-up the funds for expansion.

Customers
In many businesses, customer orders are accompanied by a deposit. If this is customary in your industry, take advantage of it. I know of one retail store that always took a 30% to 50% deposit with each customer special order. Examination of the books showed that there was $35,000 in deposits on hand at all times. This represented about 30% of the total investment in the business, and it was supplied interest-free by the customers.

Conserving Start-Up Capital

Helping to get dozens of people into business with short capital has taught me a variety of ways to reduce the initial investment. Somewhere along the line you pay, but as an optimistic entrepreneur you know that the important thing is to get going. That means using leverage, spreading the thin available cash into as many down payments as possible, the continuing payments to come out of future profits.

One of the heaviest initial investments is in leasehold improvements. Often the landlord can be prevailed upon to make the improvements and charge a higher rent. It takes a bit of selling, but I have worked this angle often. After you have made such an agreement, negotiate a graduated rent that starts low the first year or two, then increases sharply in later years of the lease. The first two years are the most hazardous for a new venture, and you will give yourself an extra cushion if you can make the heavy payments when you are over the hump.

Don't overlook the SBA lease guarantee. For a fee, the SBA will guarantee your lease, giving you the same status as a large AAA-1 concern. With this margin of safety for the landlord, you are in a better position to make a favorable deal.

In a few cases where leasing was simply not available and I found it necessary to purchase land, equipment, or facilities, I was able to work out installment payments with a balloon note. Note that I said in a few cases, because it required someone who was really hungry to sell me. This type of contract calls for low payments for several years, then a huge lump-sum payment at the end. The assumption here is that the purchaser will be financially stable at the termination of the contract and/or will refinance the purchase for an additional term.

Finally, there are some seemingly piddling resources that can add up. Use your Bankamericard or Master Charge card to the limit for personal purchases. Similarly, use your department store revolving charge accounts. You may free up several thousand dollars that can be invested in your business.

Sources of Capital in The Ongoing Business

Some of these thoughts probably belong under the heading of good management. I see them as capital resources for the small enterprise. Before a client with a going business starts seeking help in the money market, I ask him to look at ways to free up money from within. The best bet is inventory turnover. Often, the owner is the purchasing agent or the purchasing agent is also the marketing manager and head of janitorial services. The ultimate sin is being out of raw material or consumer merchandise, and the combination of pressures usually produces purchases in lumps instead of in a flowing manner. In most of the cases I have examined, judicious control of the flow of goods into the firm can reduce inventory by as much as 25% with no adverse effect on sales or deliveries. Check your inventory and see what a 25% reduction will do for available capital.

It is a rare small firm that can carry its own accounts receivable. This is well understood, and most retailers use credit cards or commercial credit companies. Manufacturers may factor their accounts. Surprisingly, even with these resources available, accounts receivable find their way onto the firm's books. Perhaps it is a rush order or a sale to a friend or relative. I am often amazed to find the owner of a retail establishment with sales volume in the $200,000 bracket having $3,000 to $5,000 in receivables past 60 days, while failing to take trade discounts because he is short $3,000 to $5,000 in cash.

If you have a short term problem that causes a profit decline, putting you in a cash flow bind, you might try a different approach to your friendly banker. Ask him to temporarily suspend principal payments on your term loan. It's surprising how easy it is to obtain agreement if you can show that the decline is temporary. This is particularly true if the cause is environmental, as during a recession. If you have real courage, you might even ask the landlord for a temporary rent reduction. He would probably rather oblige than have an empty building.

This is only a thought-starter chapter. If you look around, there is money hiding everywhere. You are in business for yourself because you are an innovator. You're not a grey-flannel-suit-type with a button-down mind and a banker who is too hot, or too cold, or too. . . .

Additional Information

1. Ted S. Frost, *Where Have All the Wooly Mammoths Gone?* Parker Publishing Co., Inc., 1976. The entire book is fun and informative. Chapter 21, "O.P.M." is about leverage—how to use other people's money.
2. Gilbert N. Dorland and John Van Der Wal, *From Idea to Maturity.* Capital Services, Ltd., 1976. A good book for more sophisticated new ventures. The authors are practitioners and offer a good deal of information on how to obtain venture capital.
3. Donald M. Dible, *Up Your Own Organization!* The Entrepreneur Press, 1974. (Paperback) See section three, "Ali Baba and the Forty Money Sources."
4. Gordon B. Baty, *Entrepreneurship: Playing To Win.* Reston Publishing Company, Inc., 1974. Chapter 15, "The Next Round of Financing" is great for going concerns looking to expand or sell out.
5. Bank of America. *Financing Small Business.* Small Business Reporter 13, 1976. Excellent guide for developing a loan package. Available free of charge at any Bank of America branch office. Or send $1.00 to Small Business Reporter, Bank of America, Department 3120, P. O. Box 37000, San Francisco, California 94137.

6. THE FRANCHISE RELATIONSHIP

There is a question as to whether a discussion on franchising belongs in a book on independent business because the nature of the franchise contract severely restricts the activities of the franchisee. It restricts his right to select his own location, to use his name in connection with the business name, to sign a corporation to the contract, to negotiate his own lease, to alter the store design, to set his own working hours, to select the product mix or service style, to vary the company image, to sell the business to whomever he pleases, and in many cases to pass the business on to his family when he dies. Such restrictions do not constitute independence, but they are not necessarily bad, for an additional right the franchisee gives up is his inalienable right to fail.

Ideally, the franchiser brings to the relationship a tested and proven product or service, substantial entrepreneurial skills, a talented management team, adequate capitalization, and a successful record.

The franchisee brings a desire to join the venture, to be independent, and to profit by his own efforts. He might also bring a willingness to work long hours and to comply with the methods of the franchiser, and adequate capital to get started.

The franchiser licenses the franchisee to conduct a business using the franchiser's trade names and business style. The franchisee pays a fee for these privileges.

The franchiser specifies a place of business, type of store, office, or facility, and all details of the business image. The franchisee agrees to accept these choices of the franchiser.

The franchiser contracts to provide a variety of cradle-to-grave services and either products or product specifications. He insists on adherence to his procedures. In many cases, he specifies every detail of daily routine. He does this in the name of continuity of image and standardization of quality. The franchisee pays a royalty fee for the services provided.

In all too many cases, either or both parties bring to the relationship deceit, lack of ability, unwillingness to focus on individual needs or organizational goals, and in the case of some franchisers, just plain fraud.

Unquestionably, there are strong advantages to buying a good franchise. If you are a neophyte in the business, you will get all the training you need. Some franchises are so powerful and have been proven so thoroughly that there is a 99 per cent chance of success as opposed to a high failure rate for independent ventures. Further, if you wish to sell out, a proven franchise will command a much higher price than will an independent business because of the continuity of management through the franchiser.

But don't get caught in the myth of independence. You will be required to do most things by the numbers, under pain of having your franchise revoked.

Assuming that you have worked through all the independence versus security problems and have made the decision to buy a franchise, what should you watch for, and what actions should you take? The first thing to do is to get a pamphlet on franchising with a check list of how to evaluate one. Good pamphlets are available from the International Franchise Association, Washington, D.C., the Small Business Administration, and the Bank of America, and franchise data can be obtained from the United States Department of Commerce. Then, you might consider some of these ideas:

.. While there are no federal laws governing franchising, most states have franchise laws. Get a copy of the law in your state, and read it for degree of stringency and coverage. If it is a tough law and a franchising company qualifies to do business in your state, you have one measure of security.

.. Don't believe that acceptance of you by a franchiser means they have evaluated your ability to get the job done. Some franchisers would select a corpse if rigor mortis had not set in and if it clutched in its hand a certified check for the amount of the franchise fee. Do your own introspection and decide if you can handle the franchise.

.. Do not deal with profit projections or average profits. Insist on actual financial statements from a cross-section of franchisees. Then, evaluate your expected return on investment.

.. Get the financial statement of the parent company and evaluate its ability to provide the services it promises.

.. Read the franchise contract. It should be simple, frank, and fair, with complete disclosure, not an instrument of repression. After you think it through with your head, listen to your gut and determine if the contract fits you.

.. Finally, and perhaps most important of all, is evaluation of the franchiser's management team. You should do this from two aspects—their managerial ability and their humanness. If the management does not measure up to good corporate standards, you will not get the profits you seek. You may turn out to be O.K., but they can bring you down.

What is the franchiser's attitude toward his franchisees? Does he see them as things to be used and exploited, or does he see them as human beings with whom he can collaborate in a life-long venture? Remember that you are going into this business to enrich your life as well as to make money. There are many franchisees with psychosomatic illnesses who have found they invested their life savings only to trade one bad job for another. One way to avoid this problem is to have lengthy interviews with as many existing franchisees as possible, quizzing them about their experiences in the relationship as well as the business aspects. Remember that franchising is a very tight, long-term contractual arrangement and, as in a partnership, you will want to weigh your commitment before it is made.

Additional Information

1. Harold Brown. *Franchising: Trap For the Trusting.* Little, Brown and Company, 1969. Condemned by franchisers as an overstatement of the ugly side of franchising. If you read this and still go ahead, you will have done your homework properly.
2. Robert M. Dias. *Franchising: The Investor's Complete Handbook.* Hastings House, 1969. Dias is former president of a franchisee organization and presents a complete picture of how to choose.
3. Robert M. Rosenberg and Madelon Bedell. *Profits From Franchising.* McGraw-Hill Book Company, 1969. A good picture of the industry by the president of a major franchise company.
4. Robert Metz. *Franchising: How To Select A Business of Your Own.* Hawthorn Books, 1969. Another helpful guide to selection.
5. *Directory of Franchising Organizations.* Pilot Industries. (Paperback) An annual directory.
6. Kenneth J. Albert. *How To Pick The Right Small Business Opportunity.* McGraw-Hill, 1977. Chapter 11, "Selecting A Franchise Opportunity," is complete and up to date.

7. FORMS OF ORGANIZATION

Most businesses are organized as sole proprietorships, partnerships, or corporations. There are other types such as limited partnerships, but they are for very special purposes and don't warrant consideration here. A variety of factors will determine which form is best for you—size of your business, if expansion is planned, liability protection you need, how public you want your affairs to be, and more. Advantages touted for some forms may turn into disadvantages. As we shall see, a good deal of thought needs to go into organizational choice.

THE SOLE PROPRIETORSHIP
This is by far the most common form used in small business. It requires no special legal agreements. You can begin anytime and end anytime. It's all yours. When you walk away from your job and start your own sole proprietorship, you keep all the income, you control every facet of the business, and whatever you do is between you, the Internal Revenue Service, and state and local authorities. As long as you have the required licenses, if any, and pay the required taxes, they don't talk, so you can do your own thing in your own way, being as secret about your business life as you desire.

Paradoxically, the same advantages also become disadvantages. To go it alone means no one will share management decisions with you. Quite often, the sole proprietor gets so deeply into the trees he is unable to view the forest and does not know when outside assistance is needed. Owning it all also means owing it all. The indi-

vidual form has unlimited liability. That means everything you own is always on the line, whether it is in the business or not. If the business fails, you can be forced to sell your house, car, and other possessions to pay business debts.

On balance, the sole proprietorship is the best way to start if what you have in mind is a simple business that does not require outside investors. The decision to incorporate can be studied at any time in the venture's life and need not be made in the beginning.

THE PARTNERSHIP

A form of business to be avoided wherever possible is the two-person partnership. While it is true that the partnership form works just fine for major law firms, accounting firms, and the like, it has too much on the down side to recommend it for most small ventures. So I don't unbalance the whole presentation, here are some partnership advantages: Two people can complement each other. One may be sales-oriented while the other partner may have production know-how. A partner brings additional capitalization to the venture.

The creation of a two-person partnership (or a two-person corporation) is usually done with only business aspects being explored. In fact, it is a relationship that is equally as demanding as the one with your wife or husband, only without the lovemaking. All such relationships begin with vows of foreverness and mutual profit. But the pressures of a growing business are more than most relationships can handle, and the usual direction is downhill. When it comes time for the divorce, the headaches really begin, as the partnership is a lot more difficult to dissolve than a marriage.

There are several other rarely considered hooks. Partners may agree that for the first few years they won't take any money other than their agreed salaries out of the business, allowing surplus to accumulate for expansion. Tax laws require that each partner report his share of the income. So, if there is a profit and it's not distributed, each partner will need to come up with cash to cover his tax liability.

Then there is the unlimited liability problem we encountered in the sole proprietorship, only in a partnership all members are fully liable. If the business goes belly up and one partner declares bankruptcy, the other is 100% liable, even if his portion of the partnership is only 10%.

If you still insist on going into a two-person partnership, at least have an adequate legal agreement. Spell out in detail who does what, and how. Limit discretionary purchases of one partner. Unless you specifically limit such actions, your partner can buy whatever he wishes without consulting you. Write a buy-and-sell agreement into the contract that clearly states how the business will be valued if one partner wishes to sell out. Finally, provide for mandatory sale to the surviving partner and have the business purchase insurance so the heirs can be paid off, or you may find yourself in business with your former partner's rotten kid.

THE CORPORATION

Most often, when we think of corporations in the United States, we conjure up the image of publicly-traded big business, billions of dollars in sales, and thousands of employees. A corporation can also be capitalized at $500 and be owned by one person. To really evaluate the corporate form, it is necessary to understand that it is a separate legal entity entirely apart from its owners. A corporation may be bought and sold in its entirety or in pieces, its stockholders may die, and still the corporation remains. In big business, this is quite obvious. No stockholder dips his fingers in the corporate till. Accountants and bookkeepers watch over its wealth. The small business person must understand that ownership of a closely held corporation carries with it exactly the same responsibilities as those for a public one. No mixing personal and corporate funds. Officers are registered with the incorporating state. The corporation files its own tax returns, and the only way money gets out of the corporation and into the hands of its stockholders is through salaries or dividends. All of this is done under close scrutiny, through a mass of paperwork.

One prime advantage of the corporate structure is its limited liability. The corporation as an entity is only liable to the limit of its assets, which means your home, car, and other possessions are safe if your business is incorporated. Well, maybe they are if you have been very careful to keep the affairs of the corporation at arm's length from your own, have kept the minutes of the meetings of your Board of Directors, and have faithfully complied with corporate rules and regulations. If someone really wants to get at you personally through a law suit, the corporation may not necessarily be the protection you thought it to be. A further myth about liability limitation explodes when you ask for a loan. The bank will want your personal signature guaranteeing the corporation. In theory, the corporation is a protective shield. In practice, the protection may vanish. To have a corporate structure do its intended job for you, retain a competent attorney and have him keep the corporate books in current condition.

Another advantage of the corporation may be in taxes. That's a complex issue, one much too involved for this book. You need a competent tax attorney to advise you about salaries versus dividends, accumulated earnings allowed, etc. If you've grown to that point, you certainly won't want to play the tax angles without expert advice.

One of the most important advantages of the corporation is transferability of ownership and multiple ownership. If you have other people involved, the only form to consider is the corporation. It allows stock to be apportioned according to various kinds of contributions. If you're figuring on leaving the business to your family intact when you die, consider incorporating.

To sum up: By incorporating, you get limited liability, possible tax advantages, ease of transfer of ownership, unlimited life span. You give up privacy, taxes may go higher, the paperwork burden goes up, and the original cost of incorporating and maintaining the corporation must be considered.

The decision about which form to take becomes highly individual, but some things I have learned may be of help to you:

If retirement benefits are important to you, check the current laws on individual (Keough) plans. There was a time when a small corporation provided superior retirement benefits, but liberalized laws now help sole proprietorships.

With a corporation, you can elect a fiscal tax year. Doing so eliminates a huge hassle at the end of the calendar year and gets you more personal attention from your accountant. You can elect a Subchapter S corporation which gives you all of the advantages you seek in a corporation while allowing you to be taxed as an individual. If you expect to incur losses the first few years, this can be very helpful. Check with your attorney and accountant.

When forming your corporation, be sure your attorney uses a 1244 Stock Plan. This is a simple procedure and allows you to take an ordinary loss (rather than the usual capital loss) if you close out the corporation. I once set up a corporation, invested services and money in it, and later decided to abandon it. The ordinary tax loss write-off came in very handy.

If you plan on selling stock to investors at some point in time, issue your own stock well in advance. Sometimes, the Internal Revenue Service looks at the lower price you may pay as taxable bonus for services. You may avoid this by allowing a time span between issues. As with all points such as this, check carefully with your attorney.

A final word: Take the most simple, direct route. You should have some overriding reason for incorporating—substantial personal assets to protect, many investors involved, or complex tax issues that can best be resolved through the corporate form.

Additional Information

1. Patrick R. Liles. *New Business Ventures and the Entrepreneur.* Richard D. Irwin, Inc., 1974. See chapter on "The Legal Forms of Business Enterprise." Excellent coverage for the growth-oriented business.
2. Ted S. Frost. *Where Have All the Wooly Mammoths Gone?* Parker Publishing Company, Inc., 1976. Chapter 18, "Two, Four, Six, Eight: Let's All Incorporate," claims that corporations are audited by the IRS more often than sole proprietorships.
3. William D. Putt, Editor. *How To Start Your Own Business.* The MIT Press, 1974. Chapter 9 is written by an attorney, Edward A. Saxe, and explores the entrepreneur and corporate laws.
4. Ernest W. Walker, Editor. *The Dynamic Small Firm: Selected Readings.* Lone Star Publishers, Inc., 1975. (Paperback) Chapter 4 by William M. Stroud covers 1244 stock.
5. Richard H. Buskirk and Percy J. Vaughn, Jr., *Managing New Enterprises.* West Publishing Co., 1976. (Paperback) Chapter 12 covers Subchapter S corporations in easy reading.

PART II
MANAGING THE SMALL ENTERPRISE

In Part I you learned some of the essential steps of getting free. Part II contains information you need to *stay free*—ways to manage your business that will keep you competitive and assure your survival.

In Chapter 8, "Maximize Your Strengths," you will find some thought-provoking ideas about specialization. In "Low Budget Advertising" you will find out how to enjoy the "creative you" on the path to greater profit. The "Cash Flow" chapter shows in simple understandable language how to deal with your checkbook and bank balance.

You will be surprised to find you can get some of the finest consulting help available—free! Have a look at "Where To Get Help." In the same chapter you can learn how to use specialists such as accountants and lawyers without feeling intimidated.

At the end of each chapter are additional sources of information that will help you to be fully informed.

8. MAXIMIZE YOUR STRENGTHS

Small business failure is most often attributed to poor management. The functions of management are most often defined as planning, controlling, and directing. In various portions of this book I address myself to these specific areas. But, before one can begin to operate as a manager there is a pre-requisite: *Know thyself.* Know your strengths, know your weaknesses, know what you expect from your business. Vague concepts and broad definitions won't do. You must constantly go deeper and deeper so that you can understand yourself, enabling you to maximize your strengths.

WORK YOUR NICHE IN LIFE

When you are an employee, company policy is dictated, and you squeeze yourself and your capabilities into corporate parameters. In a business of your own, you are free to create the business and its likeness in any way you choose. Every entrepreneur is creative. Just getting a business started is a highly creative endeavor. The new entity that you create is unlike any other. Even if it is modeled after an existing venture, it has elements about it that are uniquely yours. In the early stages, you are likely to appreciate your creation and follow your intuition in planning merchandising or marketing programs.

The problems appear when the business is well under way, when you are pushing to hurry the crossover process into profitability. Under pressure, you may begin to listen to advice or attempt to emulate success patterns of the giant enterprises. At this point, you are in danger of losing touch with the very strengths that will assure your success.

One of the real traps for the small business person is in following the competition. Big businesses utilize specialists with tunnel vision to concentrate on one facet of the business. This makes them real experts in narrow areas. The small business person is a management generalist and must see things and events in much broader perspective. In order to maximize your strengths, you should not be talked out of, or talk yourself out of, doing your own "thing."

To protect yourself from this trap, begin now to recognize and focus on your strengths.

Start out assessing your strengths by developing written answers to these questions:

1. *My Personality*—What are the traits I feel make me successful in my relationships with other people?

2. *My Life Experiences*—What are some of the things that have happened in my life that I feel have strengthened me?

3. *My Education*—What have I learned, formally and informally, that has strengthened me?

4. *Important Others*—Who are the people that have a significant, positive impact on my life, and how have they done so?

5. *My Professional Attributes*—What are the things about me I feel have made my present success possible?

6. *My Interests and Hobbies*—What else do I do well? How do these talents and activities strengthen me?

7. *My Philosophy of Life*—What do I believe about the meaning of life and my relation to it that has strengthened me?

Next, prepare a qualifications summary. List all functions of a business that you are able to fulfill. Some of these qualifications may come out of your own life, family raising, or hobbies, but they apply well to business life. Now, select the functions that you most enjoy. Can you see a distinct pattern developing? Ask yourself the question, "When do I feel most alive?" Write a detailed answer.

You now have a number of pages that identify strengths and qualifications and that pinpoint the business activities you most enjoy. Be sure you design your enterprise around this knowledge of yourself. In all of the business successes I have seen, the entrepreneur was doing what was satisfying to him, in an atmosphere he enjoyed.

If you allow yourself all the pleasure you can get from your business, all the motivation you need will be intrinsically available to you. When you are joyous about what you're doing, the energy radiates throughout the company and is felt by your customers. If you are living a life of "shoulds," your unhappiness will show through, and that, too, will be picked up by everyone.

You can never learn how to treat a customer. You can only learn how to treat yourself and then the customer will feel it. *Being* a fully functioning person is infinitely more productive than learning how to *do* something to someone. So, write your life script the way you want, not in a way that you "should" do it, and you will surely be successful.

A student was planning a moped business and the group got into a discussion of how two different people would maximize their strengths by making their individual niches in such an enterprise.

Jack is a young, energetic man who enjoys the mechanical aspects of all vehicles, likes to race anything, and prefers to spend most of his time in conversation with people. When he designed his new moped business he emphasized the high performance aspect of his line. He attracted groups of young people who formed moped teams for outings and competition. His van could be seen at all the gatherings where he did on-spot repairs, sold accessories, and enhanced his personal image in the field.

Behind the scenes operations for his business were handled by an accountant team who advised him on purchasing and on various management functions.

Doris is a young women with a strong accounting background who likes figures, finds pleasure in detailed planning, and is generally a conservative person. She organized her new moped business as a money-saving transportation device, helpful to the ecology and conservation of energy. Her customers tended to be slightly older. All business was transacted inside her store. Doris hired a personable women to handle sales while she devoted herself to overseeing the broad aspects of the business.

Here we have the same kind of business, organized in two completely different ways, each designed to maximize the strengths of the individual owners.

THE ADVANTANGES OF FLEXIBILITY

Jack B. was the owner of a new high-quality gift store in a small shopping center. Across the street was a big shopping center; and the anchor was Bullock's, a major department store chain. It was Jack's first Christmas in business, and he had worked diligently assembling a fine giftware collection.

One of his items was a group of candles shaped like vegetables and packaged in cans. The labels were colorful, price in the range of $2 to $4 each. He had an attractive display utilizing a supermarket cart. Across the street, Bullock's also had this item, and they set up a huge display with several carts.

By December 5th, Jack knew he had a winning item. Sales of the canned candles were up to several dozen per day and climbing. His initial order had been modest, but he had a back-up order placed. When he realized the second order was too small, he got on the telephone to the manufacturer and doubled the order.

On December 12th it appeared that everyone in the community was eating canned vegetable candles. Jack decided to have a look at Bullock's and see if the chain store was doing as well with this item as he was. When he arrived at the gift department the display was gone—not a candle in sight. Over lunch, the Bullock's buyer explained that he had a predetermined purchase amount for the season that was set up by the department vice-president at headquarters. When the gift buyer phoned in and asked to have a re-order placed on the candles, he was informed that his purchase allocation was filled and that he could not re-order on this item.

Back at the store, Jack got on the phone once again and ordered 100 dozen canned vegetable candles to come by air freight. As it turned out, the canned candles made Jack's Christmas season.

What's the point of this story? Big business grinds slowly. Their purchases must be planned in advance and, once committed, are difficult to change. The small business manager can quickly alter plans or change direction.

The small retailer has many advantages in flexibility. One of the most important is how he uses his display windows. When a product becomes hot or a display goes stale, he can create new excitement within hours by re-designing the window, while his counterpart in big business must wait on the schedule of the display department.

Be aware of the rigidity built into big business planning. Take advantage of *your* flexibility to create sales. This axiom goes for any type of business. A small manufacturer can take bigger risks on the downside of a product's life-cycle, squeezing out continuing business because he can alter a product line more quickly than his highly automated, less flexible, big business competition.

KEEP IT SIMPLE

The real strength of small business is in the personal, human contact between the owner and his customers or clients. There is nothing as important to a customer as being able to talk with the boss, and no one can ever sell as well as the boss. Woe unto the business person who removes himself from his customers by putting himself behind a fancy desk and closed doors.

As the business grows and the money is available, the desire to emulate fancy corporate surroundings is almost irresistible. It is well to remember that lettered parking spaces, deep carpeting, and the key to the executive washroom are passed out in lieu of more meaningful things that the corporation cannot provide, and that you already have, such as freedom.

Peter H. started with a backyard operation and in a few years had an amazingly successful chain of stores. The way he showed his growing affluence was to purchase a radio-equipped Mercedes-Benz. As he got more involved with similar "toys," his business began to decline.

Peter is a bright, young man, and one day he realized that he had lost all the important contacts with his employees and customers in his pre-occupation with things. Recently he was driving a Volkswagen bus that does double duty as a delivery vehicle. His business has recovered nicely, and so has Peter.

In retail businesses, super-slick atmospheres often create a feeling of intimidation or alienation that is the property and problem of big business. Many small firms survive simply because they bring humanness back into the business transaction. A cold, impersonal, museum-like atmosphere is the least desirable image a business can project.

A client of my consulting firm sent me to visit one of his stores. Little signs around the store said "Please Do Not Handle The Merchandise." Everything in this store was spotless and in perfect order.

He might as well have put up a sign telling customers not to come in. I suggested he take down the signs and not be quite such a perfectionist in his housekeeping. It was interesting to observe customers respond positively to the more relaxed atmosphere.

DO UNTO CUSTOMERS

I am almost embarrassed to write this portion of the book because it all seems so obvious. Yet, everyday I see small business persons handling their customers in an uncaring way that would make them frantic if they were treated in the same manner. I keep watching these many obvious mistakes, wondering what these owners are thinking about.

One evening I visited a new neighborhood restaurant. Care had been given to create a comfortable atmosphere, and the food was quite good, considering the newness. But, it all went out the window with the service. It seems that one of only three waitresses had not shown up, so the cocktail waitress was pressed into serving food. The place became crowded and things went very slowly and unpleasantly. The owner was wandering around tending to absolutely unimportant details. He must have known that the proper thing for him to do was to take orders, look to customers' needs, and in any way see that they were happy so that they would return. Yet he persisted in ignoring the reality under his nose.

Just up the street is a restaurant that is part of a national chain. The waiters are young college men who have been instructed exactly how they are to behave. The service is fast; but unfortunately this style only partially works, and often smiles appear to be painted on. The food is adequate but boring. This was our entrepreneur's competition. The restaurateur's strength is in his personal touch. He could leave his individual stamp on the business and get close to his clientele. But, somehow he failed to recognize his advantage. Instead of maximizing his strengths, he played into the hands of his chain competition. In less than six months, he was out of business.

This is only one of countless examples to be seen everywhere. In order to succeed, you must examine your priorities. Whether you are in manufacturing, service, or retailing, your first job is being with your customers in a personal, caring way.

THE IMPORTANCE OF SPECIALIZATION

Perhaps this section should be called "ultra-specialization" to emphasize the importance of concentration on a narrow specialty rather than trying to cover the whole field. This is particularly true for retail stores or service businesses in large urban areas. While big business needs to capture a massive portion of the market, a finely tuned small business can prosper in a very tiny market segment.

These are some of the very successful specialty businesses that have concentrated on a narrow product line or service:

. . Old fashioned cookie shop. People will pay $3.00 per pound for chocolate chip cookies when the product is tops and the environment inviting.

. . Yogurt shops are the newest fast-food craze.

. . Skateboard parks provide a place for kids of all ages to enjoy their sport off the street.

. . Plant leasing and service.

. . Hamburger stands. McDonald's made a few dollars at this specialty.

. . Pants stores. The one with the name I like is "The Place Where You Go To Buy Pants, Inc."

. . Fireplace stores got a huge boost with the energy crisis.

. . "Athlete's Feet" is doing a great job selling gym shoes.

In addition to the obvious opportunities created by new technology, there are new business concepts in the growing trend toward humanism. Anything that tends to individualize or personalize sells. As long as it is not mass-produced, people want it.

This list could go on for pages. The point is that by being a specialist you carve out a corner of the business world where you can become important.

Going the ultra-specialization route has some advantages in addition to marketing:

. . Specialization dictates concentration of your purchasing, making your firm more important to your suppliers. This concentration pays great dividends where special purchases have become available or when you need credit extension.

. . Generally, you need less space to do the same dollar volume.

. . Salespersons become experts, and everyone likes to buy from someone who knows his product thoroughly.

. . The creation of a business image is simpler, more effective and less costly.

. . Customers will seek you out if they know that you have substantial expertise in one area.

.. Specialization encourages the use of proprietary brands which tend to produce higher profit margins.

.. You can actually become "the world's best" in a concentrated field.

There is a pitfall in all of this emphasis. Watch out that you don't concentrate on a fad or build an image in a fading style.

I recall an operation of the early 1960s which began in New York City and spread to other parts of the country. It was a time when inexpensive contemporary furniture was made of wood frames and fabric covered foam slabs. The very popular line sold by a firm ballooned into dozens of retail outlets, both company-owned and franchised. When foam rubber furniture went out of style, the company was left with no place to turn. So before you specialize or name a business in a specific way, do enough market research to determine the life-cycle of your product.

Additional Information

This small business concept does not appear in traditional sources. It derives from my experience as a practitioner and consultant. To improve your understanding of this material, pick out some businesses that appear to fit the standards you would like to set. Then, make an appointment to visit the proprietor. You'll find successful people receptive to sharing, and perhaps you will learn something of value. You are certain to be inspired by this effort.

9. SMALL FIRM MARKETING

Marketing is the heart of a business venture. A product is useless until it is sold; a service never begins until someone contracts for it. Whether your business is a one-person brokerage, a large retail operation, or a small craft manufacturing company, the primary focus of your effort is on getting the product or service sold.

MARKET RESEARCH

Market research is often seen as too complex for small firms. In reality, there is a vast array of information and simple techniques that can generate meaningful data without using a computer or other fancy tools.

Ideally, market research should be approached using the best scientific methods. In practice all the small business person can do is to be as scientific as possible. This means striving for objectivity, obtaining the most accurate measurements possible, and investigating all the facts fully.

There are two types of data: primary and secondary. Primary data is generated by the small business person himself. It can include surveys, analysis of customer lists, etc. Some types of primary market research are:

.. Test Marketing

This can be done in many ways. Prototypes of a new product can be shown at a trade show and orders taken. The response will indicate the potential for the product. Before going into full production, a short run (even if it is costly) of the product can be made and tested in one or several local outlets, or by one sales group. Market testing is a form of market research that can indicate the size of effort and investment to be made in a new product.

.. Internal Record Data

If your firm keeps complete records, they can provide amazing information. Studying addresses of customers (or phone number exchanges) can define the trading area draw. Credit records used in charge accounts can yield data about size of family and income. Service and manufacturing firms can use records to analyze sales in similar ways.

.. Observations

Just counting traffic produces information. License plate numbers in parking lots may provide information about the locale in which customers reside. Simply changing displays and studying and recording customer reactions provides useful data.

.. Surveys

These can be done by phone or by questionnaire and can provide data on product preference, shopping hours, new service or product introduction and a host of others. University professors and doctoral candidates can be very helpful in designing surveys.

Secondary data can be found easily through a variety of sources. It is important in using secondary data to completely understand the time and circumstances under which it was gathered before applying it to your business. Much of it was prepared for uses other than your own and you must be adept at analyzing it for your benefit.

The government is a vast source of secondary market research data:

.. The United States Department of Commerce, Department of Agriculture, Department of Labor, HEW and others are a storehouse of market statistics and other business information.

.. The Small Business Administration can guide you to data they collect. The *Marketer's Aids* published by SBA can be helpful in many ways.

.. The United States Census provides a comprehensive view of an area including population, dwelling count, income levels, family growth patterns, number of retail establishments, volume of business by individual trades, household expenditure patterns, and more.

Private sources provide a variety of secondary market research information. Some is available as a public service without charge; some can be quite expensive:

.. Original research studies such as those provided by Stanford Research Institute and Battelle Memorial Institute cover specific industries. They work for their client firms, but often major banks provide these and other studies for their customers. Stockbrokers have research information on many industries and companies.

.. The reference librarian at your local library can help by referring you to abstracting services, dissertations, monographs, specialized bibliographies, patent documentation, and technical digest services.

.. Books and texts, particularly those by the American Management Association, contain much useful research.

.. Trade association meetings and trade shows are loaded with information about new technology, business sources, and promotional studies.

.. Major banks publish business trends and forecasts, in general and on specific businesses and industries.

.. Business supplier organizations, such as National Cash Register Company, publish retail statistics. Your local telephone company provides a variety of statistical information.

SELECTING LOCATIONS

The choice of location for a small manufacturing firm is usually based on suitability for the manufacturing process, price, and availability of labor and transportation. For service or retail businesses dealing direct with the public, location choice becomes much more important and complex. Finding the right site is an exhaustive process and should not be shortcut. Take all of these factors into consideration:

1. *Accessibility of Location*
   Can customers find you easily? Is there adequate parking? Does public transportation serve the area adequately? Can you receive merchandise and make deliveries conveniently? What is the future of the area?

2. *Traffic Flow*
   Foot traffic is the most valuable; but often counting auto traffic can be helpful if it stops or slows in front of your location. Walk the area during the day and at night and have friends do the same. Collect all the data and make an evaluation. Remember that the number of persons passing the location is not as important as who they are. Obviously, a traffic pattern consisting mostly of men will not benefit a women's clothing store.

3. *Location of Competitors and Compatible Businesses*
   Each business has its own needs. Automobile businesses are better clustered on an "auto row," as people tend to comparison-shop. A specialty store can often depend on the traffic generated by a department store, even when some of the merchandise carried is competitive. Similarly, you can benefit from the traffic drawn by heavy advertisers.

   A few rare businesses are able to generate a following of their own because of uniqueness or price advantage. Most often it is advisable to be in a visible location within a known shopping center or area.

4. *Condition of the Premises*
   Consider the cost of remodeling. Expensive work in old structures may put you into a position where your investment cost will be too high. Does the building help convey your image? Does the layout of the space lend itself to your style of business? Examine the window display space carefully. This is a

most important consideration for retailers. A bulkhead that is the wrong height can make attractive displays impossible. How costly are utilities? Old buildings are expensive to heat and air-condition. Finally, what of the future? If you have on-site storage space, could it be converted to display space in an expansion move?

5. *Making The Right Lease*
Lawyers examine leases for specific legal aspects. Don't depend on yours to advise you if the lease is okay or not. You need to know:
.. Is the rental a fixed amount or is there a percentage clause? If there is a percentage clause (most good leases have one), is it the correct amount for your type of business? If you negotiate price, try working the percentage down rather than to reduce the fixed amount. In the long haul, this will serve your interest better.
.. Be sure that the stated business you can conduct appears in the broadest terms possible. As times change you may need to alter your merchandise mix. If the lease is too restrictive, your flexibility will be hampered.
.. Services or utilities payments, yours or the landlord's, should be fully spelled out, e.g., who maintains the air conditioning system?
.. Who pays for what insurance? If the landlord carries certain types of coverage, this can be an important cost saving.
.. Does the lease carry a cost-of-living increase? What will this mean in the years ahead?
.. You should be able to sublet the premises in case of a future move. Freedom to do this in the lease is important.
.. The length of the lease requires serious attention. The tendency for new entrepreneurs is to make short term leases in order to limit their financial exposure. In many cases it is desirable to have a long term lease in order to protect your position. A good idea is to state exactly the termination date of the lease, rather than having it expire at the end of a five- or ten-year term. A retail business with a heavy Christmas season involvement should have a January 31 termination. This allows full advantage of the Christmas business, plus a a good sale month in case of moving or close-out.

6. *Major Shopping Center Leases*

Leasing a location in a major shopping center requires special considerations. Often such leases are made while the center is in the planning stage. It is usually the responsibility of the tenant to completely construct the space he will occupy, which makes this a large scale investment. If you do decide on a major center, you can have the same negotiating power as a large chain through an SBA lease guarantee (see the chapter, "Where To Get Help").

On the plus side, large centers offer heavy foot traffic which encourages impulse buying. Most centers have co-operative advertising, a known location and adequate parking.

On the minus side are high rents, forced contribution to center maintenance, mandatory association dues, complex leases. One of the most important privileges you lose is that of setting your own hours. Store hours are mandated in the lease of large centers.

Check out neighboring stores carefully. Centers present a variety of images ranging from high-quality, high-fashion, to low-end discount. Make sure that your image is compatible with that of the center. Beware—many centers take years to develop. Large chains expect to lose money in the first few years. Most small businesses cannot afford this luxury. You are cautioned to examine large centers thoroughly before signing on.

PRODUCT DECISIONS

It is surprising how many new products come into the marketplace and fail. Often, a minimum of market testing would have suggested changes in the product or influenced a decision to delay or avoid market entry. This is not new knowledge, and most inventors or entrepreneurs intellectually understand the process of market testing.

The basic problem is an emotional one. The discovery of a process or the design of a new product requires total involvement. After months of creative effort, the tendency is to fall in love with the product. With this degree of commitment, it is very difficult to pay attention when data tells you your product has little or no marketability. It is somewhat akin to telling a woman her child is ugly.

Recently, a young man was referred to me by some of my colleagues at the university. He had collaborated on a book that had taken several years, and he was exuberant about its ability to change and improve lives. He had written a book previously and was disappointed in the way it had been promoted by the publisher, so he had decided to go into the publishing business and promote the new book through his own organization. He came to me seeking advice about how to form his business and how to secure financial backing.

As I listened to his story unfold, it seemed to me that his strength was in his creativity and many of his problems might be solved by finding a publisher who would agree on promotional activity that would satisfy the author. This would free his energy from business and allow him to maximize his creative potential. Throughout the conversation, he continually interrupted to tell me how fantastic the book was. I finally persuaded him to engage in an exercise where we looked at the book as a product to be bought and sold, not as a work of art. Seeing your product on two levels, the creative level and the business level, is very difficult. In order to enjoy the creative aspects it is often necessary to step outside yourself and view the business portion in a detached manner. It is the sound business decision that will enable you to go on and enjoy greater creativity.

PRICING FOR PROFIT

For a general overview of pricing policies in your industry, it is wise to consult the trade organization, speak with suppliers, and check out competitors. Basic pricing policy varies widely, depending on whether you are in manufacturing, retailing, or service. Some of the source material at the end of the chapter will help you with basics. In this section it is our purpose to go beyond basics and explore some pricing concepts and techniques that will help you create satisfactory profit margins and avoid head-on price competition with big business.

Watch Your Competition

Good advice. You should always watch your competition, but not so you can meet their prices, only so you will know what to do to out-perform them. Sometimes, it pays to raise your prices to beat competition rather than lower them. Let's look at some examples:

Ken C. is a hairdresser. As with many of the fine beauty

salons in California, he also cuts men's hair; and I have gone to him for years. Originally, he had a small shop of his own and the price for a haircut was $8.00. Later, he sold out and went to work in a more fashionable area. I followed him, and the price was $12.00. Recently, he opened a super fancy establishment with a multitude of services, and his price is now $18.00. This jump has little to do with inflation or with his increasing expertise. It all has to do with the style and ambiance of the shop. In the new place, he would probably do less business at a lower price.

Recently, I worked with a group putting together an organization that will deliver educational seminars on a group of subjects just now coming into vogue. When we priced out the costs involved, we concluded that the organization would be profitable selling the seminars for $150 per admission. When we researched the market and the nature of our clients, we concluded that we would attract more buyers at $250 than at $150 because the lower figure appeared too cheap for the quality of the program.

This type of pricing is replicated many times over in the business world. It represents the best of small business planning—wherever possible, find a niche that is yours and work it, avoiding the pricing rat-race that will get you caught between the giants.

Merchandising For A Price Advantage

Those of us on the inside of business become very aware of the widespread availability of certain products or the similar nature of services we purvey. We often make the assumption that the buying public has the same awareness. Particularly in retailing, this may be an erroneous assumption and force us into profit-reducing price competition.

See if this is familiar: You are away from home on a business trip or vacation. You go browsing in interesting shops and find several items that you would like to own or to give as gifts. Sometime later you become aware that these items have been available in a number of stores in your own town, but you had never noticed them. The presentation made all the difference. You may have even paid a higher price because the item was made to appear of higher value by association with other goods in the display.

There are many ways to be different. Sometimes, it involves grouping diverse products by color in a display. For a manufacturer, it may mean grouping into a package for ease of selling or cataloging items in a unique way. Creative merchandising is a way to avoid the price competition of the larger corporations.

> The giftware section of a large women's fashions chain on the west coast has an unusual and successful merchandising policy. Whenever possible, they create their own packaging, combining color or utility. One successful item combined four of the same style coffee mugs, each a different color, in an interesting box. The box was displayed in a jewel-like individual setting. This item had preference in treatment because it carried a substantial markup. Another part of this store's unusual policy is to select carefully, make substantial initial purchases, then never reorder or repeat an item. This keeps them in the forefront of fashion.

Creating the illusion of exclusivity can be done with private labeling, minor alterations to the product, and display techniques. It can sometimes be done in cooperation with suppliers. The very nature of the creative planning and the motivation required makes this a viable pricing option for small business.

Magic Prices
This information is primarily for retailers, although manufacturers of consumer goods also find thoughtful choice of price points helpful in assisting their retailers. The first choice to be made is price endings. Prices such as $29.95 and $79.95 make an impression different from $29.89 and $79.89, or $30.00 and $80.00. Considering the level of sophistication of the buying public, small retailers are well advised to try even dollar pricing. This is something you can experiment with and alter to suit your clientele.

There are some choices that are clearly important. You will come to know the general price areas for your business, but within your range watch for mistakes like these: If your cost on an item is $16.00 and the traditional markon is 100%, you would be led to a price of $32.00. In the vast majority of stores, a price of $29.00 or $29.95 will produce a great many more sales. In this instance, you would be taking a short mark-up in order to work with a popular price point. If the item cost $18.00, you might be inclined to go for a $35.95 or $36.00 retail. In this instance, a price of $39.00 or $39.95 will most likely produce more sales. Here, you can actually improve the sales of an item by raising the figure to a popular price point.

By moving toward these popular prices, you will also tend to eliminate the confusion of choices that is created by a variety of prices. So, think about a pricing policy, try for price points that work and try to eliminate in-between prices that confuse.

Pricing Promotions and Sales

The small business person's best promotional possibilities come about through offering obviously unusual values. Seemingly, this statement would apply more to the giants, since they have all the advantages of being able to work with shorter profit margins and to purchase for less in quantity. However, there are two aspects reserved for the small business that make a great deal of difference.

The first advantage is in the purchasing agent. The large corporation has a purchasing department, usually under rules and regulations. Purchases require advance planning, and there are huge time-lags between orders and the movement of goods.

The small business owner is most often directly involved in purchasing. He may range wherever he wishes, with no restrictions, and is free to find new resources at any time. I have seen small business owners at the shipping docks going through packing crates in order to make special purchases on imports. The typical corporate buyer waits in his hotel room for someone to bring him samples. The twin attributes of motivation and flexibility make it much more likely that the small business person will find bargains.

The second advantage is in small quantity purchases. In order to feed large production plants or huge retail outlets, the giants need substantial quantities of a given item. The small business owner can work with odd lots and special purchases, enabling him to create promotions that offer outstanding values to his customers, often retaining better-than-average profit margins.

A small textile manufacturer made placemats, napkins, aprons, and the like for the giftware and housewares industries. The majority of the products were silkscreened at a company-owned facility. Searching for new products and ideas, the owner contacted a large national fabric manufacturer and learned about a substantial quantity of fabrics available as mill ends. There was an array of high-priced material, but only 50 yards of some, 100 yards of others. He made the purchase and put together a line of tote bags that could be sewn in his own facility. The bags were snapped up by retailers who then promoted "limited quantity bags made of fabrics by famous designers, at half-price."

For the alert, small business person, the availability of "deals" like this are endless. They allow you to outprice others, and they are simply not of interest to your giant competition.

DISTRIBUTION THROUGH MANUFACTURER'S REPRESENTATIVES

When a business enters the market with a new product line, the owners probably do most of the selling. As the business expands, it may be necessary to secure sales coverage on a regional or national basis.

Fortunately, this is not a problem, as a vast network of manufacturer's representatives are available to handle your sales distribution. "Reps" are independent business men or women who handle the sales for a group of manufacturers. Typically they have been employed as sales persons within an industry, know the business and territory well, and have established accounts they call on.

Reps work strictly on commission and pay their own expenses. They get paid only when they make a sale, so you incur only variable expenses, rather than maintaining your own sales force on a fixed-expense basis.

Most reps enter business for themselves for the same reason you did—to escape the rigidity of corporate life. Their motivation is high, they are self-disciplined and are usually above average in sales ability. Yet, they are not all equal, so it pays to select reps with great care.

The advantages of having a ready-made distribution system often makes it possible for a new business to get started. There are some disadvantages in working with reps. Since they are independent business persons, you do not retain as much control. They usually have established their own method of bookeeping, which means that you may need to adapt to a variety of styles.

The best way to contact reps in your industry is through trade shows or the trade association. If you introduce your product through a booth at a trade show, you will find that the reps contact you. These shows also have a special area where reps and manufacturers can get together.

PERSONAL SELLING

The critical portion of any entrepreneurial endeavor is sales, and the person best suited to make those sales is the owner-manager himself. Who is more highly motivated? Who knows more about the product or service? Who can profit most from direct customer contact? I am certain that there have been successes in unusual situations by non-sales-oriented entrepreneurs, but the risk factor increases enormously.

This concept is so central to any new venture that I feel comfortable with this categorical statement: If you don't really enjoy selling, don't go into business for yourself; or get a partner who can be on the outside while you are on the inside. Note that I said a partner, not an employee. That top selling position still needs the motivation of ownership.

The word "sales" covers a variety of activities. Some examples of not-so-obvious selling include the successful hairdresser who sells by making public appearances at women's groups or at hair-styling events. He also sells through the personality of the shop. The successful restaurateur sells by being out front to greet customers and manage the ambiance of the establishment. Certainly, the successful consultant sells services; and even the goal-oriented head of an accounting firm knows that he can't wait for business to find him.

Assuming that you really love to sell, you must watch that the mechanics of the business don't interfere with your primary function of selling. This is really tricky. You're not only chief salesman, you're chief purchasing agent, head bookkeeper, in charge of maintenance, sometimes janitor, and guardian of employee morale. Don't lose your perspective. Somehow, arrange your work priorities so that *you* make the most important customer contacts.

CREATING A SUCCESSFUL IMAGE

The large corporation creates a corporate image that has no relation to any of its employees, but in the small enterprise the business image and the entrepreneur's image meld into one. It is important that the business image not cast its leader into a role he cannot comfortably and naturally portray. Part of any early planning should be to create the kind of business image you want to project, with yourself as the center. Once you know exactly what business you are in and who your prospective customers are, you should begin to fabricate an image about your company which will relate to your target population.

An image is synthetic and can be treated or changed by a deliberate effort. It can convey any message you wish—exclusivity, innovativeness, low prices. It is wise to avoid elaborate symbols in the logo or trade style. Big organizations can afford to spend millions creating an identification with a symbol, but the small business must achieve the same results by being direct. It is always profitable to select a name that directly describes the business, and does not need any advertising to get the idea across.

When planning your firm's image, these are some points you will want to remember:

1. Watch every piece of your literature, stationery, and other public materials. Whatever your business, your customers want to feel that they are in competent hands, and your product literature, hand-outs, and other collateral material become the most important way they have of identifying with you. If necessary, spend a little more money than you had planned, but don't ignore this most important facet of your public image.

2. Plan your packaging to sell. Whether it's a wholesale or retail product, your packages are seen by a great number of people. Be sure you don't miss the opportunity to build your image this way.

3. The decor of your offices, showrooms, service area, or retail store is extremely important to your image. It does not have to be plush and expensive—that may be exactly the wrong thing to do. Think out the story you want to tell. When you are sure you know, then start out carefully to select the furnishings and accessories to create the image you want. Furniture and office stores supply interior designers without charge. If you are using hand-me-downs, consult some of the design magazines on how to place them to achieve the best effect. *Better Homes and Gardens, Apartment Life,* and others are full of inexpensive ideas to create inviting interior environments.

4. Make your image believable. Be sure it does not convey something impossible for you to fulfill.

5. Keep it simple. Simple thoughts or actions are best to convey an image. Don't get into complications which will prove costly in the future.

6. Watch that you don't go too far. If you are conveying youthful energy, see that it does not get childlike and eliminate older people who feel youthful. Or, if conservatism is your goal, don't convey "stuffed shirt."

To sum up: Know yourself and what fits for you. Know what business you are in and who your customers are. Be sure that you and your business fit together. Then, carefully and thoroughly set out to make every aspect of your business convey your message to your customers.

Additional Information

1. Richard H. Buskirk and Percy J. Vaughn, Jr., *Managing New Enterprises*. West Publishing Co., 1976 (Paperback). Page 276 begins an excellent discussion on how to sell the mass merchandiser.
2. Ernest W. Walker, Editor. *The Dynamic Small Firm: Selected Readings*. Lone Star Publishers, Inc., 1975. (Paperback) Part IV has a series of articles on small firm marketing.
3. Lawrence A. Klatt, Editor. *Managing The Dynamic Small Firm: Readings*. Wadsworth Publishing Company, Inc., 1971. (Paperback) Page 153 begins an article, "Meeting The Competition of the Giants."
4. Harvey C. Krentzman. *Managing For Profits*. Small Business Administration, 1968. First portion is on marketing. Has a bibliography at the end of the section.
5. H. N. Broom and Justin G. Longenecker. *Small Business Management*. South-Western Publishing Co., 1975. This textbook has a good section on market research.
6. Leon A. Wortman. *Successful Small Business Management*. AMACOM, 1976. Part Three, "Marketing and Sales" covers sales and salesman well.

7. Dan Steinhoff. *Small Business Management Fundamentals.* McGraw-Hill, 1974. (Paperback) Textbook with good fundamental information on pricing and merchandising. See Part 5.
8. Charles A. Bearchell. *Retailing: A Professional Approach.* Harcourt Brace Jovanovich, Inc., 1975. Good chapter on pricing for retailers.
9. Manufacturer's Agents National Association, 3130 Wilshire Boulevard, Los Angeles, California 90005, can help you locate representatives to handle distribution of your products.

10. LOW-BUDGET ADVERTISING AND PROMOTION

Advertising is the most controversial and individual aspect of business. For most small business owners, it is also the most threatening. But, if you want to use your creativity fully and have some fun, the time spent on advertising can be the most challenging and rewarding.

While it seems rather presumptuous to question high-price Madison Avenue advertising talent, it is my contention that the in-house, low-budget production capabilities of most small businesses far exceeds that of advertising agencies. Even though you may have limited technical know-how, you are so close to the operation and so interconnected with the image, that you can actually produce better advertising than a sophisticated agency.

When you formulated your complete business plan as outlined in Chapter 2, you wrote a substantial amount about your business concept. If bankers, investors, friends, or relatives have been able to read and understand what your business is about, you are a successful, creative writer. That is just the amount of talent it takes to create advertising copy and programs.

As you continue to put together the catalogues, brochures, menus, or whatever printed or spoken material your business requires, you reinforce the creative talents that are needed for advertising. Any number of successful small business ad campaigns have been designed and implemented by the business owners.

In short, don't get buffaloed by the mystery of the ad business. You can be your own agency and turn out materials that will work very well. Start with yourself and your staff as the creative center. If you need additional help, it is available in abundance, and at reasonable cost:

.. If you need an artist, there are many freelance professionals available. Often, agency people will moonlight. Recent art school graduates can be surprisingly capable.

.. Newspapers or magazines will set type for you without charge. You can order the type yourself using the type-face books they provide. If this seems a bit difficult, use a layout person. Often your artist has this capability. Or, check with the advertising department of a local university for a student proficient in lay-out. Sometimes you can get the professor for a reasonable fee.

.. If you need copy for a radio or a TV ad, you can get agency services free. In most cases radio and TV stations will pay an agency 15% commission on what they charge you for time. This is built into the price; and if you don't use an agency, the money is retained by the station. In local situations where there is no fee, try the speech department of the university. You may get not only copy, but a voice tape which you can simply give the radio station.

.. Be sure to check with the ad media. Often newspapers, radio stations and TV stations have a complete creative staff that will design an ad or commercial to your order.

.. Many manufacturers or suppliers have advertising material that is supplied free.

.. Newspapers and magazines may supply blow-ups or paste-ups of your ad that you can use as point-of-sale aids or in creating bro-chures or mailers. This allows original make-ready to go even further.

Now that you have access to all the available creative talent, you know you can do whatever you wish in advertising your business.

Next comes budgeting and deciding which media will be most effective for you.

DEVELOPING A PROGRAM AND BUDGET

Dust off your business plan. If you are in the start-up stage, you can refer to your concept and marketing plan to help you identify who your customer is, what you are trying to sell, and the competitive advantages of your product or service. Start by developing some goals or results that you want your advertising to produce.

Your business plan should have an amount budgeted for advertising. You may want to reassess it at this time. Check industry sources, such as trade associations, to find out what portion of their budgets others are allocating to advertising. You will need to allocate the annual budget to specific time frames. If you are in retailing, you may wish to advertise heavily in some seasons and do little or maintenance advertising in others. Whatever you do, plan to spend your allocation as if it were rent or utilities. All businesses, even the one-person consulting company, need promotion.

After you have established goals and a budget, you need to select the most cost-effective media. Consider:

1. The customer you want to reach. Radio stations have selected audiences through their programming. If you have a product for teenagers, a rock radio station might be more appropriate than newspapers.

2. Your geographic area. Manufacturers of industrial products might do best in trade publications. A local specialty store would use the community newspaper.

3. Budget. An annual budget of $3,000, for example, is just not going to make it on TV.

With your general plan in mind, let's look at some of the specific advantages, problems and techniques around the media you will most likely use.

NEWSPAPERS

Newspapers are the favorite media of small retailers. They can be very effective if you make the proper choices out of a sometimes bewildering array of alternatives—

.. Which paper?
.. Which day of the week?
.. What size ad?

.. What ad style?

.. What frequency?

.. Which section of the paper?

In smaller communities, the choice becomes narrow and simple. In the big cities, these are complex questions without any one correct answer. You will need to study the situation, then do some trial runs to find out what works best for you. Just so you don't feel disadvantaged—the fancy ad agencies don't have any answers either. They go through the same process you do, only they do it with someone else's money.

One of the major advantages of newspapers is that you can make decisions and measure results fast. It takes only a few weeks of advanced planning for a newspaper ad.

A major disadvantage is in trying to reach a select audience. If you are aiming for a narrowly segmented group, it might be best to try other media, such as direct mail.

DIRECT MAIL

One of the most valuable assets of any business does not show up on the balance sheet—it's your own customer mailing list. Anyone who has been in your place of business, bought your product, or utilized your service recognizes your name and knows something about your firm. A piece of mail from you is very likely to get attention. If you are running a business that is unique, specializes, and follows the other practices we have been advocating, you can expect to get excellent results from well-conceived and well-timed mailing pieces. It is very important that you continue to build the size of this list, as the results will be directly proportionate to the number of mailers. However you do it, never fail to add to your list the names and addresses of every customer or prospective customer you contact.

Using compiled lists may also be an effective direct mail method. These are available through a variety of organizations. Consult your telephone directory, under "Mailing Lists," for the names of firms that sell mailing lists. You can buy lists that zero in on the specific demographic characteristics you seek.

Before printing brochures, postcards or folders, get several bids. Printing costs (and quality) vary widely. The heaviest expense is in the preparation. The cost per piece decreases sharply as the quantity goes up. Carefully examine the cost-effectiveness of the size of your direct mail advertising.

RADIO

Local radio can produce some surprising low-budget results. For most small ventures, radio is best utilized for institutional (image-building) advertising. It is less effective for promotion, although as your name becomes known, radio can get promotional results as well.

With radio, you can zero in on your target population directly. The type of programming determines the listening audience for any station. The demographics of each station's audience are part of their sales package and can be most helpful in avoiding the throw-away circulation associated with most newspaper advertising. A good rule to remember is that radio advertising needs to be used consistently to be effective.

One interesting aspect of radio is the availability of "deals." By combining various time segments and utilizing "flights" (e.g., on for two weeks, and off for one, etc.) special prices often become available. In smaller communities, there is always the possibility of barter. You can exchange your product for radio time. This makes your actual cost considerably less.

MAGAZINES

Magazines, particularly special-interest magazines, have a long life span. You can utilize high-quality printing to polish your image. Generally, magazine space is expensive and must be prepared months in advance.

Magazines have very specific audiences. Information about this and circulation are available through the publication's sales department. Most national magazines have local editions with special pages for the areas in which they are circulated. Costs of these are surprisingly low. Even if you are a small firm, you might be pleased to find you can advertise in a highly respected national magazine.

PUBLIC RELATIONS

This is another area of mystique perpetuated by the grey-flannel-suit (or whatever they're wearing now) crowd. Most people believe that getting free publicity requires knowing the "in" people, greasing the right palms, and driving a Jaguar. Not so! If you are just the least bit venturesome and reasonably literate, you can get the type of publicity that will pay off in profits.

A substantial portion of the material in many publications, particularly trade journals, actually consists of press releases. They can be recognized since they refer to a particular product, service, or person and do not carry a by-line of one of the publication's staff. Information about a product that appears as a news story often draws more reader response than an ad because it seems to have another person talking about it. Well-timed press releases can be effective aids to a promotion.

Here are some ideas that will help you put out your own press releases:

1. Remember that you are writing a news story. Don't try to write ad copy. Keep your story brief and factual. Well written short articles have a better chance of being printed than long ones. Use plain paper, double-spaced. Put the release date at the top. Use of a catchy headline is important. Read some of the publications you might want to print your release, to find examples of good copy.

2. If your release lends itself to illustration, include a glossy photo or art work.

3. Write a cover letter to the editor with any additional information you would like him to have. Let him know you're the owner of the business. This carries weight in the trade. Be sure to thank him for printing your article.

4. At the library, check *Standard Rate and Data.* It lists every magazine in the U.S. You can select the ones that are likely to bring you most benefit.

5. When is a good time to send out a release? Any reason will do—introduction of a new product, when you sponsor events, opening of a new store or manufacturing plant, anything with human interest.

6. If all this frightens you, but you still think it's a good idea, get some help from pros (but not the high-priced ones). Journalism professors at local universities will often be happy to help you for modest fees. Local newspaper people often freelance on their own time.

There is enormous potential in press releases, and the results can be far out of proportion to the cost. Imagine having news stories about your company appear in hundreds of publications in one concentrated period of time. It can be done if you don't get trapped into thinking PR is only for the big boys.

The whole subject of advertising frightens many small business persons, and they either don't attempt any or overspend to get results. If you are creative enough to get a business started, you can have productive advertising within your budget. Stretch your potential and be surprised!

Additional Information

1. Cynthia Smith. *How To Get Big Results From A Small Advertising Budget.* Hawthorn Books, 1973. Very good coverage of the subject. A good reference manual to have on hand.
2. E. Joseph Cossman. *How I Made $1,000,000 In Mail Order.* Prentice-Hall, 1963. Packed with how-to information for the neophyte.
3. Philip Ward Burton and G. Bowman Kreer. *Advertising Copywriting.* Printice-Hall, 1962. Good hand book.
4. John V. Petrof, Peter S. Carusone and John E. McDavid. *Small Business Management: Concepts and Techniques for Improving Decisions.* McGraw-Hill, 1972. See Chapters 15 and 16 for good coverage of the managerial aspects of planning, organizing and controlling the advertising function.
5. Lawrence L. Steinmetz, John B. Kling, Donald P. Stegall. *Managing The Small Business.* Richard D. Irwin, Inc., 1968. See Chapter 22, "Advertising—Waste or Wisdom."

11. UTILIZING THE FINANCIAL STATEMENTS

No one can be a success in business without keeping accurate records and understanding the financial statements they produce. Show me someone who won't get interested in figures and I will lay heavy odds on his failure. It's that important.

For years I have tried to understand why so many small business persons will avoid the figure portion of their enterprise. My best explantion is that our educational system fails to educate and that the accounting profession creates fear in order to perpetuate client dependency. The system does the same for lawyers. Instead of simple and direct language, we get legalese that requires expensive interpretation.

At the moment I don't see how we can beat the system; but I am not about to let any accountant run my business, and I hope you won't either. So, in order to be in control and have the accountants work for us, it is imperative to understand at least the managerial aspects of financial statements. If you hang in with me, I am going to try and explain financial statements in this chapter, and cash flow in the next, in a way that you can understand and apply. I will be using the accountant's language so that you can communicate with him, but the concepts come out of experience and through everyday use. I promise you that once you have learned to analyze your financial statements and utilize the knowledge they produce, you will be exhilerated by the sense of control this capability will give you over your business life.

BASIC RECORD KEEPING

In order to develop a meaningful financial statement, it is important that you have a good basic record-keeping system, and that you allocate expenses systematically. While it's possible to develop a system of your own, this is one place where I would employ the knowledge of an accountant or bookkeeping service. The days of keeping scraps of paper in a shoe box are definitely over. The government has seen to that with its complexity of required forms. Such haphazard measures will make it very difficult for you to prepare your income tax returns, and they will obviously not provide any managerial assistance at all.

There are many simple pre-designed systems. Since your accountant will be developing statements from your basic records, it is well that you jointly decide on the system to be used. I have managed a half-million dollar retail store with ten employees and kept all the basic records by myself in one-half hour per day.

Your system will have a number of expense accounts, and you will need to decide which expense goes where. Most of these decisions are clear cut, e.g., salaries, office supplies, rent, interest. Examples of some that can be sticky are travel, contributions to local business groups, window signs. Should insurance on the truck be charged to vehicle expense or to the insurance account? Whichever way you decide is not important. It *is* important that you remember what you did, and that you are consistent. Attention to input details will help a lot in the development of accurate financial statements. The two statements that will concern you are called the INCOME STATEMENT (also called PROFIT AND LOSS STATEMENT, or simply P & L) and the BALANCE SHEET.

If you really want accurate control of your business, have financial statements produced monthly. At the absolute minimum get them quarterly. This is a really important point. You need statements often, and as close to the end of the reporting period as possible. It won't do you any good to get a year-end financial statement in March. Remember that one of the main competitive strengths of small business is its flexibility. Get your records to the accountant on time. Then insist that he turn out a statement for you in ten days. By the fifteenth of the month following you should be reviewing the progress of your business for the preceding period.

TIPS FOR SIMPLE RECORD KEEPING

Your life will be a lot easier if you keep your records as simple as possible. Have all the information you need to make intelligent decisions about your business, but watch out for accountants who want to install fancy systems that you don't understand. Here are a few simplification hints that have worked for me.

.. Try multiple voucher checks. The bottom portion of the check shows what the payment is for, discounts taken, and the accounting classification the expense is to be charged against. The original can go to the payee without additional explanation. The second copy becomes your check register, and the third copy can be attached to the payee's invoice for permanent filing.

.. Keep each transaction in one cradle-to-grave file. A purchase of merchandise for a retail store is a good example: Start with a purchase order. When the merchandise is received, check it in against the supplier's shipping copy and your purchase order. Match these two with the invoice and "OK" for payment. If there has been any correspondence about this shipment, keep it attached to the file. Similarly, damage claims or other matters stay with the file. Finally, when the invoice is paid with a multiple voucher check, one copy of the check is attached. The completed file may also include notes about pricing or any other pertinent information.

.. Write checks for everything possible and deposit all receipts in the bank. Set up a petty cash fund with vouchers, but use it only for very small expenses.

.. Take inventory quarterly; count and price it accurately. Financial statements based on inventory estimates aren't worth much.

THE INCOME STATEMENT

The P & L shows how much your company makes or (horrors) loses in the time period covered by the statement. It matches the amount you received from selling your goods or services against the costs of operation. The result is profit or loss. In addition to your work of allocation at the basic level, other managerial decisions will effect the outcome of the statement: how you value inventory, doubtful accounts, and method of depreciation. So, stay aware of what you have done when it is time to analyze the statement.

Examine Exhibit 1, the P & L of Sampson's Furniture Store for a twelve-month period. If we were analyzing this statement, we would begin by comparing it with the statement for several prior years. We would be looking at how much sales increased, how the gross profit margin held up or improved, and how well we were holding expenses in line. This comparison would go on, line for line, and by the time our analysis was complete, we would have notes about questionable data, areas we needed to improve, and the beginning of our short-range planning for the coming year.

To complete our analysis, we would compare our statement to similar ones in the furniture industry. Composite figures for stores like the example, in the $500,000 annual volume range, are available for retail stores from Dun and Bradstreet and National Cash Register Company. The Bank of America *Small Business Reporters* (see additional information at end of chapter) also provide data on selected businesses. Another source of comparative data is often available through the trade associations for your industry.

You will note that figures indicating the percentage of gross sales have been entered for key expense items. Utilizing Dun and Bradstreet figures and the Bank of America Small Business *Reporter on Home Furnishing Stores,* we can draw these important inferences:

1. The gross profit ratio of this business is 42% of sales, which is at the high end of reporting stores. This would indicate that Sampson's is doing a good pricing job, and having few mark downs. We could further infer that in order to achieve this high gross margin their merchandising policy is working.

2. The advertising figure of 4% is at the low end of the spread for like stores and, since the sales and profits are reasonable, the advertising budget is probably doing an effective job. A question that might be asked in planning for next year is "What would happen to our sales if we increased our dollar advertising budget?"

3. The total salaries of 13% are 1% higher than similar stores. This calls to the owner's attention that he needs to cut this expense, or increase sales while holding salaries at their present level.

4. The net profit of 7.6% exceeds the industry range of 4.5% to 6%, which tells us that this store is doing an adequate all-around job.

A great deal more analysis is possible, but this will give you an idea of the wealth of information that is available in a P & L statement.

STATEMENT OF INCOME

Sampson's Furniture Store
January 1, 1978 to December 31, 1978

SALES	$506,000	
COST OF SALES	293,480	58%
GROSS PROFIT	$212,520	42%
DIRECT EXPENSE		
Sales Salaries	55,660	11%
Advertising	21,850	4%
Freight In	34,960	7%
Total Direct Expense	$112,470	
GENERAL EXPENSE		
Other Salaries	$ 12,200	2%
Bad Debt Expense	300	
Credit Card Expense	1,150	
Depreciation	3,240	
Utilities	3,260	
Insurance	1,900	
Interest	1,400	
Legal and Accounting	1,800	
Office	640	
Rent	22,220	4%
Sign Lease	1,970	
Repairs and Maintenance	1,600	
Payroll Tax	4,750	
Taxes, other	1,654	
Telephone	1,810	
Travel	1,115	
Other Expense	673	
Total General Expense	$ 61,662	
NET PROFIT BEFORE TAXES	$ 38,388	7.6%

EXHIBIT 1

THE BALANCE SHEET

While the Income Statement shows operating results over a specific period of time, the Balance Sheet is like a financial photograph —it shows the condition of the business at one moment in time.

The balance sheet for Sampson's Furniture is shown in Exhibit 2. The first portion is called "Assets" and represents everything the company owns that is worth money. Assets are classified as current or fixed.

1. Current assets include anything that can be converted to cash in one year. Examples include accounts receivable, inventory, stocks, etc.

2. Fixed assets are items for long term use. They decline in value, so they are reduced on the Balance Sheet by the use of a depreciation figure. There are various choices of depreciation you can use in order to satisfy Internal Revenue Service requirements. Your accountant is a good source of advice here.

Anything the business owes is a liability. Liabilities are classified as current or long term.

1. Current liabilities must be paid within one year. They include short-term notes, trade obligations and, in the case of Sampson's, deposits from customers.

2. Long-term liabilities include long-term loans and bonds.

The equity is the owner's investment (or the dollar value of his ownership). It always equals the assets of the business minus the liabilities.

The best way to study a Balance Sheet is through the use of ratios. There are generally accepted standards that are used by bankers and investors in evaluating a company. Ratios for businesses like yours may be obtained through the same sources mentioned under the P & L analysis.

Having a look at Sampson's Balance Sheet, we can make these determinations:

Tests of Profitability

1. The first tests of profitability are gross profit percentage and net profit to net sales. We examined these on a previous page, from the P & L statement.

BALANCE SHEET
Sampson's Furniture Store
December 31, 1978

CURRENT ASSETS

Cash on Hand	$ 6,041	
Accounts Receivable	1,430	
Inventory, at cost	55,500	
Prepaid Expense	1,120	
Total Current Assets		$64,091

FIXED ASSETS

Equipment, Furniture, Fixtures	$10,934	
Leasehold Improvements	11,674	
Accumulated Depreciation	(2,070)	
Total Property and Equipment		$20,538

TOTAL ASSETS	$84,629	$84,629

LIABILITIES AND EQUITY

CURRENT LIABILITIES

Note Payable ABC Bank	$ 4,000	
Accounts Payable, Trade	7,850	
Accrued Expenses	3,760	
Customer Deposits	8,400	
Total Current Liabilities		$24,010

LONG TERM LIABILITIES

Note Payable ABC Bank	$10,000	
Total Long Term Liabilities		$10,000

TOTAL LIABILITIES	$34,010	$34,010

EQUITY

Proprietor's Equity Beginning of Period . .		$30,231
Net Profit for Period	$38,388	
Less Proprietor's Drawing	18,000	
Increase in Equity		20,388
Owner's Equity		$50,619

TOTAL LIABILITIES AND EQUITY		$84,629

EXHIBIT 2

2. A very important test of profitability is Return on Investment (ROI). This is the same figure you would want to know about the purchase of stock or if you planned to open a savings account. If you put $1,000 into a savings account, what will be the per cent of interest you will earn? The way we figure ROI is to take the net profit for the period (for a sole proprietorship we would use the figure after the owners draw, in this case, $20,388), divided by the owner's equity at the beginning of the period. These calculations produce a ROI of 53%. That's a mighty healthy figure, anyway you look at it. It says that Mr. Sampson takes a salary of $18,000 and in addition earns 53% on his investment. Figures of this type are not unusual in many small ventures.

3. Another good test of profitability is Inventory Turnover. This figure indicates how fast inventory is moving in and out of the business. High turnover requires less capital investment in the business and results in a higher ROI. It is one important measure of how good an entrepreneur is at merchandising his venture. To calculate inventory turnover, divide sales by the average inventory (the average for the year could be obtained from the average of the monthly or quarterly income statements). For this example let's assume that the $55,500 inventory represents the average for the year. Dividing it into sales of $506,000 gives an inventory turnover of 9.1 times. National averages for firms of this type and size are between 4 and 4.6 turns. Mr. Sampson is a very good merchant indeed.

Tests of Liquidity.

Liquidity represents the ability of the company to meet its current obligations. It has to do with the amount and type of current assets with which current liabilities can be met. Bankers watch these ratios at loan time and credit agencies examine them carefully in assigning the ratings that vitally effect your open line of trade credit.

1. The most common is current ratio. It best describes the margin of safety for creditors. It is calculated by dividing the current assets by the current liabilities. Again, use comparative statistics for your industry. A generally accepted guideline is that 2:1 is an adequate current ratio. Having a very high current ratio may mean that funds are not being deployed in an efficient manner. Sampson's ratio is a satisfactory 2.66:1.

2. A test applied primarily by bankers is the acid test (or quick) ratio. Calculate it by dividing quick assets (those that can be turned

into immediate cash) by current liabilities. It may take some months to liquidate inventory so this item is not included in quick ratio. Sampson's quick ratio consists of cash and accounts receivable divided by current liabilities, which equals .31:1. Most acceptable standards are 1:1, so Sampson's balance sheet is not favorable by this measure. Digging a little deeper we would know that this figure is for December 31, and January is a sale month in the home furnishings industry. Most probably, by the end of January the inventory will be lower and the cash higher resulting in a better acid test ratio.

The information provided by financial statements is vital to the management of your business. This brief chapter is intended to get you started on acquiring more knowledge. Pursue some of the readings below; or, better yet, take one of the courses offered by the U.S. Small Business Administration or the school of business of your local university.

Additional Information

1. Small Business Reporter. *Understanding Financial Statements.* Bank of America, 1974. This handy pamphlet is available from any Bank of America branch or by writing to: Small Business Reporter, Bank of America, Department 3120, P. O. Box 37000, San Francisco, California 94137. Enclose $1.00 check or money order. No cash. This will be the best $1.00 investment you ever made. I don't know of a better presentation.
2. John N. Myer. *What the Executive Should Know About the Accountant's Statements.* The Citadel Press, 1965. Written for the non-financial executive. Comprehensive coverage for the slightly larger firm.
3. Small Business Administration. *Financial Record-Keeping for Small Stores.* Small Business Management Series No. 32., 1966. Order from your local SBA office or Superintendent of Documents, U. S. Government Printing Office, Washington, D.C., 20402. Price—$1.60. Basic record keeping plus financial statement information.
4. Dun and Bradstreet. *How to Build Profits by Controlling Costs.* D & B, 1973. Available for $1.00 from your local D & B office. Down-to-earth information for the small business person.

5. Small Business Administration. *Ratio Analysis for Small Business.* Small Business Management Series No. 20, 1970. 35¢ from the U. S. Government Printing Office, Washington, D.C. 20402. How do you beat this value?

6. Lyn and Laura Taetzsch. *Practical Accounting For Small Business.* Petrocelli/Charter, 1977. Lay language and understandable illustrations to help you with your bookkeeping and understanding your accountant.

12. CASH FLOW

I remember when, as a young entrepreneur, I first made the amazing discovery that the profit I made in my business and the amount of money I had in my bank account had very little relationship. One year I made a net profit of $35,000 and still was short of cash to pay my current obligations. With the help of a crash course in cash flow and a friendly old accountant, I learned that a rapidly growing business could get into as much financial trouble as one that was failing. That's an amazing fact—many *successful* firms go out of business because of poor financial planning.

Understanding cash flow (the accountant's term) is simple when you relate it directly to your checkbook. That's all cash flow is about—the flow of cash into your bank account and the relationship to the amount of the checks you write. Just as you must control the other facets of your business, you must also control the flow of cash so that you will be able to meet all your obligations as they come due.

With a little reflection, the wide disparity between profit on a P & L statement and cash in the bank becomes understandable. A successful retail store, for example, might show great profit on a statement, but increased business requires carrying more inventory, which ties up cash. Remodeling and new equipment might be required, which takes cash. If the store has charge accounts, the influx of cash lags behind sales. Without careful planning, this store could grow right out of business.

The way to avoid running out of cash is to make regular cash-flow forecasts. When it appears that shortages will occur, management decisions can be made intelligently. These might take the form of postponing purchases, arranging better terms, or short-term borrowing from the bank. If borrowing is needed, it is far better to arrange a loan well in advance than to call on your friendly banker after you run out of cash.

DEVELOPING THE CASH FLOW FORECAST

Cash-flow forecasting (or budgeting) is simply a matter of listing how much cash you expect to come in and how much you expect to go out in a given period of time. It is best to make forecasts regularly and on no less than a three-month basis. If you can look ahead six months to a year, it is most helpful. If you are creating a new business plan, it is essential to forecast for two years.

Income statement planning is an integral part of and precedes cash-flow forecasting. It is best to begin with income statements from the previous years. Analyze the progress of the business. Study general business conditions now and the outlook for the period covered by your forecasting.

Begin by forecasting your sales. Remember that increases (or decreases) will not develop evenly. Sales for each month will depend on your growth rate, the general business climate, inflation, and your individual promotional efforts.

Once you have projected sales, project cost of sales and expenses. These items will probably increase if you are projecting a sales increase. The result of your work will be a forecast income statement.

Exhibit 3 is a sample form for creating a three-month cash-flow forecast. Using the information from the income-statement forecast, you can begin to develop how the cash will come in and go out as the business proceeds. If your average collection period is forty-five days on accounts receivable, that is when the cash will show up. Make all the entries of cash receipts and total.

Estimate when payments will fall due on all the expense items in your income projection. Don't forget that inventory purchases will come in hunks, not in a smooth flow, so it is essential that you have accurate knowledge of shipping schedules and invoice due dates. Loan principal payments should be carefully entered.

Your calculations will start with a beginning cash balance, add cash receipts, deduct cash payments and conclude with an ending cash balance.

The example form includes space for your forecasts and the entry of actual figures. When you have made a number of forecasts and compared with the actual reality, you will become more and more accurate.

No matter the size of your business, if you use cash forecasting as a regular part of your management control system, you will enhance all of your decision-making. If every owner did this, I am certain that the small business success rate would be substantially higher.

CASH FLOW FORECAST for 3 months ending _____

	JANUARY		FEBRUARY		MARCH	
	FORECAST	ACTUAL	FORECAST	ACTUAL	FORECAST	ACTUAL
Beginning Cash Balance						
Cash Receipts						
Cash Sales						
Accounts Receivable						
Other Income						
Total Cash Received						
Cash Payments						
Inventory Purchases						
Payroll						
Payroll Taxes						
Rent						
Utilities						
Advertising						
Sales Taxes						
Other Taxes						
Asset Purchases						
Supplies						
Loan Payments						
Other						
Total Cash Payments						
Ending Cash Balance						

EXHIBIT 3

Additional Information

1. Ernest W. Walker, Editor. *The Dynamic Small Firm: Selected Readings.* Lone Star Publishers, Inc., 1975. Chapter 14 by James Holtz covers cash budgeting and forecasting.
2. Leon A. Wortman. *Successful Small Business Management.* AMACOM, 1976. Chapter 16, "How Much Cash Do You Need?" provides good coverage of the subject.
3. Small Business Reporter. *Retail Financial Records.* Bank of America, 1971. Has a chart for planning cash flow that you can utilize directly. Order from Bank of America, Department 3120, P. O. Box 37000, San Francisco, California 94137. Enclose check or money order for $1.00.

13. PLANNING FOR PLEASURE AND PROFIT

The enriching, rewarding life is all in the "here and now." Living in the future is fantasy. I like to be in the now as much as possible, to savor each moment, to be as completely present in mindbody-spirit as I can. The discussion of planning seems out of sync with this attitude. However, if we don't do some real planning for our business, we may not be around to enjoy some future "here and now."

Too much of small business managing is done by use of the financial statement or, worse, by seat of the pants. A financial statement is a historical document, often too old to be of value in steering your business. If you are set up for monthly statements and are quite efficient, you may get the raw data to your accountant by the 10th of the month. He assembles it, feeds it into the computer and, if you are really lucky, gives the statement to you by the end of the month. If you study it immediately, you are 30 days behind material that was accumulating for an additional 30 days. Even when things go perfectly, you are looking at figures that are from 30 to 60 days old. This tells us fairly conclusively that the only way to manage a small business is to utilize the financial statement as one of the elements in forecasting and planning. For the purpose of our discussion, forecasting involves figures and is generally short range, one to two years. Planning is around life strategy and is most often medium to long range.

WHYS AND HOWS OF FORECASTING

Each person who cooks or cares for a household engages in forecasting. It involves keeping a running list of supplies and food that is needed on hand (stock) and materials that are needed for upcoming specific menus. An inadequate job of forecasting means either running out of supplies or having too many, resulting in spoilage or an overloaded cupboard. The more proficient one becomes, the more likely the household budget will be effectively utilized.

In any business, the center of forecasting and planning is the marketing function. How much of what goods or services are we going to sell in a given period? This is not a time to engage in wishful thinking. Good sales forecasting utilizes eyes and ears beyond the standard two each. Begin with history. Examine your figures for the same period in past years. Then analyze today's market conditions nationally and in your specific area. Your trade association and trade publication can be very helpful in supplying trends for your industry.

Once you have made your sales projections (usually for a year), don't lock them in concrete. Re-examine and alter them as often as necessary in the light of changing conditions. It's important to be aware that sales projections are not only for budgeting purposes—they also serve as goals for your own and/or your staff's sales efforts. If you are involved with investors of any type, you have probably already learned that failure to meet profit projections is relatively easy to explain away because of expenses you failed to forecast correctly; but it is really difficult to obtain approval of failure to meet sales projections.

The projection of expenses involves careful calculations, but all of the variables are hooked into your projection of sales. Many of my clients who formerly worked from financial statements or intuition find it really exciting to completely work through a set of profit forecasts and then use them as a guideline for the daily functioning of their business.

TOOLS OF FORECASTING

In earlier chapters you learned how to project a profit and loss statement and a cash flow statement. These projections are made on a regular ongoing basis and provide the working tools to guide your venture. You might consider adding one more—the break-even analysis. Your accountant can provide a formula for making this simple calculation. Its function is to tell you whether your sales production figures have resulted in a profit or loss, on a daily basis if you wish. As you become more proficient with the tools of forecasting and their use, you will begin to enjoy the energizing experience of being in total control of your business.

LONG-RANGE PLANNING

For large corporations the business of long-range planning involves economists, futurists, computers, and often a complete staff which does nothing but work five or ten years in the future. For small business persons, it is about all they can do to get out a set of one-year or two-year forecasts. Still, it is important to dream the impossible dream, so our long-range planning starts with day dreaming. It sounds strange, but the plague of bigness is its inertia, which makes adaptability to change extremely difficult; and the inevitability of change is a significant fact of our economy. The innovative, adaptable small-business owner, as the sole decision-maker, can effect change more rapidly. He can safely confine long-range planning to ethereal stuff that will take him where he wants to go with his whole life.

As I said earlier, I try to live in the "now," but I find it useful to set aside a period of time each week for pure fantasizing. I go off into some future time and imagine my life as I would like it to be. The realities of my present life will, of course, always dictate the direction and scope of my flight of fancy. For example, if my business is doing well, bringing me satisfaction, and if the possibilities of growth and expansion into new areas really do exist, fantasies come quickly to mind. These fantasies get picked over, and some of them become the foundation for further exploration.

The first time you try this free-floating exercise, you may be surprised how difficult it is to bring up any imagery. Long experience in corporate or public sector bureaucracy has a tendency to squeeze out creativity and force you into tunnel vision.

In order to make your business work for you in a way that produces maximum freedom and happiness, you may need to go through a freeing-up period. In the quiet state that you set aside for yourself, just keep letting go of rigid concepts or anything that keeps you bound to traditional forms of what to do and how to be. As you transcend old boundaries, you will begin to know the steps you need to take in order to keep moving towards your goal of a whole-person business.

While all this may hardly appear to be sound business advice, I believe it is. Whenever we move towards those goals that are most meaningful to us, we release a great deal of energy. It is this free flow of energy that makes for real success.

Once you have some long-range concepts that integrate your needs with real possibilities, you can begin to translate them into shorter-range plans that will lead to eventual completion.

Additional Information

1. John V. Petrof, Peter S. Carusone, and John E. McDavid, *Small Business Management: Concepts and Techniques for Improving Decisions.* McGraw-Hill, 1972. Several excellent chapters on marketing strategy, planning, budgeting and break-even analysis.
2. The Small Business Administration has blank forms to assist you with profit and cash flow forecasting.
3. Harry Gross, *Financing for Small and Medium Sized Business.* Prentice-Hall, 1969. Very detailed book on financial planning for a growing business.
4. David Markstein, *Money Raising and Planning for the Small Business.* Henry Regnery Co., 1974. Good overview of financial planning.
5. Ernest W. Walker, *The Dynamic Small Firm.* Lone Star Publishers, 1975. A book of readings. See Part II, Strategy and Planning.

Van Ginkel & Moor

14. WHERE TO GET HELP

In order to make your venture economically viable and personally satisfying, you will want to have as much knowledge as possible. It *is* available to you, but not always in the most easily assimilated form. Much needs to be done to provide a readily available, complete assistance program to small business.

In this chapter I am going to point out some of the agencies and places where help is available. It is virtually impossible to do this in detail, but I assume that if you get pointed in the right direction, you can make the steps by yourself. It is very easy to get caught up in the busy life of business ownership and avoid seeking help when you need it. But, with a little patience and perseverance, you will find that many experts are available to assist you, often at little or no charge.

U.S. SMALL BUSINESS ADMINISTRATION

This agency was set up to serve your needs in four major areas: financial assistance, investment assistance, management assistance, and procurement assistance. There are approximately 127 other federal programs that provide assistance to small business, but SBA is your home base. Whatever you need to know, you can find the answer or direction through an SBA counselor. With all this potential, it is amazing how many small business persons do not avail themselves of SBA services. Don't be one of them. The people at SBA are professionals, and they want to help you. There are 96 field offices. Check your phone book for the location nearest you.

Management and Technical Assistance

This is high priority in the SBA. Management Assistance Officers provide counseling, design and initiate training programs, and coordinate all facets of management assistance. They would normally be your initial contact at an SBA field office. Management assistance programs available to you free, or at nominal cost:

1. SCORE/ACE. The SBA's Service Corps of Retired Executives (SCORE) and Active Corps of Executives (ACE) are successful women and men who volunteer their time to assist you, free of charge. They will help you analyze your problems and offer advice leading to successful business ventures. Imagine the pool of talent that is yours for the asking, in the counseling center near you, or in your own place of business.

2. SMALL BUSINESS DEVELOPMENT CENTERS coordinate the educational resources of universities and a number of federal agencies to make one-stop assistance available to small business in technological, financial, managerial, advocacy, and marketing areas. This is a fine program, and if there is an SBDC in your area (check with SBA) you should become familiar with its services.

3. SMALL BUSINESS INSTITUTE (SBI) utilizes college and university faculty and students to assist small business operators in areas of operations, growth, and stability. You may be assigned a team of three or four students, under direction of a professor, who will consult with you for a complete academic term. They will give you a written report of their findings and recommendations and assist in implementation if you wish—all free.

4. CALL Contracts program provides professional management consultants to economically or socially disadvantaged small businesses. Requests for these services can be made at an SBA district office and are free to the client.

At the present time SBA is putting special effort into helping women and minorities become small business owners and assisting small manufacturers in exporting.

Training Programs and Materials

SBA conducts and co-sponsors a variety of management training courses, conferences, and problem-solving clinics for small business. They are taught by seasoned practitioners or professors. There is a nominal charge for some courses, others are free to attendees. These programs change to meet local needs, so call the nearest SBA office for current information.

If you are just preparing to start in business, don't miss the SBA Pre-Business Workshop. It is held periodically to examine such important foundation aspects as tax regulations, insurance requirements, good management practices, and other start-up topics.

Looking for specific types of information? Free literature is grouped under these headings: Management Aids For Small Manufacturers, Small Marketers Aids, Small Business Bibliographies, and Counseling Notes. Call the local SBA office and ask for SBA Form 115A. You can then order literature by dialing toll-free, 800-433-7272; or, in Texas, 800-792-8901.

For a nominal price, you can obtain any of 30 booklets devoted to special management concerns. If you're starting a new venture there may be a booklet about your specific type of business. Call the SBA for Form 115B, complete it, and send it to the United States Government Printing Office at the address provided.

Financial and Other Assistance

Don't forget all the financial assistance available through SBA. Among these are direct and guaranteed loans, lease guarantees, disaster loans, and economic opportunity loans.

SBA provides procurement assistance which aids small manufacturers and service companies. Technical assistance is also available.

U.S. DEPARTMENT OF COMMERCE

The explicit mission of the U.S. Department of Commerce is to "foster, promote, and develop the foreign and domestic commerce of the United States." There are main field offices and branch offices close to you with a wide variety of services. You will find an extensive library of government and private reports, directories, and periodicals that can be helpful to you in everything from marketing to technology.

If you are in foreign trade, the Bureau of Export Development will assist you in every conceivable way, including having a trade specialist visit your plant, securing representation for you at International Trade fairs, listing your products, and more

Another branch of the U.S. Department of Commerce, the National Technical Information Service, is the central source for the sale of government-sponsored research, development, engineering reports, and other analyses by Federal agencies. There are over

400,000 research reports on file that you may obtain. For a booklet covering all the services, write to National Technical Information Service, 5285 Port Royal Road, Springfield, Virginia 22161, or contact the local U.S. Department of Commerce office.

COLLEGES AND UNIVERSITIES

Most institutions of higher learning, including community colleges, four-year colleges, and universities, have extension departments, continuing education or adult education centers. They offer a wide variety of business courses, many specifically for small firms. By contacting these institutions, you can get on their mailing lists and will receive notification of all the courses and seminars they put on. Often the opportunity to get together with local business persons and discuss issues of mutual interest is worth the price of admission.

Many business school professors do consulting work. If you find someone with practical background and current academic status, it's likely he is up-to-date on the world of work. Do a thorough screening process, checking references as you would for any employee, and you may find yourself with some extremely valuable help at a very modest fee.

TRADE ORGANIZATIONS

Every business fits into the realm of a trade organization, and it can be enormously helpful to you. Ordinarily, there is a trade publication that keeps you updated on your industry and supplies valuable information through articles, press releases, and advertising. The editor is an excellent source of information, and letters to such persons usually bring prompt replies. Most trade organizations sponsor seminars or conventions. In addition to speeches, papers, and various presentations, the hallway and after-hours exchanges are often stimulating and thought-provoking.

PUBLIC LIBRARIES

What is this doing in here? Everyone knows about the library. Yes, but do you really use it as a first source of information? Here are just a few of the things you are likely to find in a U.S. Government Depository Library:

1. Complete U.S. Patent files. Use these to check out inventions that may be useful in your business.

2. Periodicals in most major industrial categories, particularly journals such as *American Journal of Small Business* and *Journal of Small Business Management.*

Directories provide a host of information about companies, products, people. These are important ones:

1. *Poor's Register of Directors and Executives* will lead you to the contact person in major organizations and provide you with important biographical data.

2. *Moody's Industrial Manual* tells you a company's size, products, top executives, and details of the corporate structure.

3. *Who's Who in Commerce and Industry* leads you directly to the industrial bigshots.

4. *Thomas' Register of American Manufacturers* will help you locate the source of brand names, provide you with sources for your own goods, give you size and details of the company you wish to contact.

5. Trade directories of various kinds will lead you to purchasing agents.

6. The *Wall Street Journal* and other business publications keep you current with the economy.

All these publications are available in nearly every public or higher education library.

OTHER PUBLIC AGENCIES

Programs of education and sources of information for the small business person are available in abundance through federal agencies such as Office of Education (HEW), Department of Labor, Department of Agriculture, Department of Transportation, Federal Energy Administration, National Aeronautics and Space Administration, and Bureau of Census. The best way to keep tabs on these is through your friendly SBA office.

One organization, the National Science Foundation, funds major research projects all over the country. Some are particularly applicable to small business. One such project in process is particularly interesting, The Experimental Center for the Advancement of Invention and Innovation. This center, with the mouthful name, is devoted to getting new ideas off the ground through research, planning, and development—the same type of thing that big corporations do through their own research and development departments. Nothing like this has been available to small business persons. For more information, write The Experimental Center for the Advancement of Invention and Innovation, College of Business Administration, 131 Gilbert Hall, University of Oregon, Eugene, Oregon 97403.

This is certainly not an exhaustive list of sources, but any one of them can provide you with specific information or update your skills, leading to greater stability and profit in your business.

WORKING WITH SPECIALISTS

Experienced professional assistance may appear expensive but, with proper selection and utilization, it is a wise business investment. The owner-manager of a small business is a person with extensive and diverse responsibilities, often without experts or staff to aid him. He is faced with a variety of issues that require substantial knowledge, and he may not have the managerial tools or skills to handle them. Professional consultants can often be the answer.

Probably the most important aspect of your work with specialists is to continually update your own knowledge so you understand the data you receive. Many small business persons choose to simply hand over unintelligible areas of worklife to the experts and then abide by their decision. This is bound to create problems. Don't hand over decision-making. Let the experts provide you with the information you need, then make your own decisions. You will be amazed to find that most experts do, in fact, know the details of their specialty; but your ability to make business decisions may be superior to theirs. There are two key areas where specialized assistance is well advised—legal and accounting/finance.

Attorneys

Small business persons are confronted with problems in such diverse areas as general corporate law, tax law, contracts, labor negotiations, litigation, pension plans, and security regulations. New and changing federal and state laws continually create new legal problems. Your lawyer can also assist you with the initial legal form of your business, suggest methods of capitalization, and help with credit problems.

If you have no problems requiring a high degree of specialization, seek out a general-practice lawyer. He should have proven ability and charge a fair fee. It's probably best not to select a friend or (worse) a relative. You lose the advantage of calling the shots and may hesitate to ask for what you want.

The entire legal profession in the United States is under scrutiny. With so many new members entering the profession, there is a proliferating number of make-work practices. The odds against finding an honest lawyer who will have your best interest at heart are climbing. You won't know bad legal advice until it is too late, so select with great care.

After expertise, the most important factor in selecting a lawyer is a match in personal chemistry. You should feel comfortable with, and be able to relate well to, this most important person on your adjunct staff. If you find that the relationship is not working, break it off as early as possible and find someone else.

Accountants

Most business owners under-utilize their accountants. They think of accounting only in terms of preparing tax statements. If you work closely with your accountant, he can help you control costs and increase profits. In the start-up phase of your business, he can guide you in making profit and cash-flow projections, and in determining your capital requirements. The design of your bookkeeping system should be a team effort.

In the on-going business, your accountant will do financial statement analysis, and, if you function well together, he can teach you much that you need to know about profit potential, budget forecasting, borrowing, and taxes.

There is nothing that will affect your business more adversely than poor accounting work. It will deprive you of the accurate figures that you need to manage all facets of your venture. So, just as you do with your attorney, use your accountant well. Continue to develop your own knowledge and figure sense so that you communicate with each other in a meaningful way.

There may be a time in your business when you consider bringing a bookkeeper or accountant in-house as an employee. Before you make such a move, examine it from many aspects. Even though hourly fees may appear high, the independent accountant has a staff that he can assign to a project when you have urgent need. It is also easier to reduce the use of fee people than to cut a regular employee.

Effective use of specialists by an aware, understanding small business owner maximizes managerial control and profit potential.

Additional Information

1. E. Joseph Cossman. *How To Get $50,000 Worth of Services Free, Each Year, From the U. S. Government.* Frederick Felling, 1972. Looking for a new product? Want to sell overseas? Cossman tells you ways to get back some of your tax money.
2. Donald M. Dible. *The Pure Joy of Making More Money.* The Entrepreneur Press, 1976. The body of the book is primarily a re-hash of *Up Your Own Organization,* but the appendix contains sources of information on American firms and a listing of directories that are useful in marketing.
3. United States Government Printing Office, Washington, D.C. 20402. Write and ask for a list of books in specific categories that interest you. Prepare to be amazed.
4. Harold Shaffer and Herbert Greenwald. *Independent Retailing.* Prentice-Hall, 1976. Comprehensive book for retailers. Lists trade journals and associations.
5. Joseph C. Schabacker. *Small Business Information Sources (An Annotated Bibliography).* International Council for Small Business, 1976. This valuable document is a guide to just about everything ever written on small business. You should have it in your library. Available through ICSB, University of Wisconsin-Extension, 929 North Sixth Street, Milwaukee, Wisconsin 53203. Price is $10.00.
6. *Journal of Small Business Management* is a publication of International Council for Small Business. Write General Secretary, ICSB, UW-Extension, 929 N. Sixth Street, Milwaukee, Wisconsin 53203. Has excellent articles of current interest and reviews of new books. If you want to really get with the small business scene, join the International Council for Small Business.
7. Howard H. Stern. *Running Your Own Business.* Ward Ritchie Press, 1976. See Chapter 15, "How To Handle Lawyers and Accountants."
8. Benjamin M. Becker and Fred Tillman. *The Family Owned Business.* Commerce Clearing House, Inc., 1975. See Chapter 9, "Consultants and The Family Business."
9. Richard Buskirk and Percy J. Vaughn, Jr. *Managing New Enterprises.* West Publishing Co., 1976. Aaron Levine authors a chapter, "Contractor or Employee?" Valuable tax information regarding independent contractors vs. employees.

PART III
WORKING WITH PEOPLE

If in your business you work with even one person—your wife, husband, child, friend, or an employee—then what is contained in these chapters is critical to your livelihood and to your life. If you are building an organization, you will learn that no matter what your technical strengths, how you deal with people will determine the degree of your success.

The key to the entire section is you, the owner/manager. There are no "techniques" to use on people. It is only your own maturation as a person that will help you to work with your people in meaningful ways.

My approach to being with people is a synthesis of three very powerful influences in my life: Dr. Jerry Greenwald, friend, therapist, author, who helped me in my own growth process towards becoming the person I was meant to be; Dr. Carl Rogers' person-centered concept started me on a new way of thinking about relationships; Dr. Jack Gibb, friend and mentor, whose TORI theory is the way I live my life and the way I create organizational environments.

15. MANAGING YOURSELF

I would like to share with you how I am learning to manage myself and, in the process, how I am becoming free.

At the age of 8, I became an entrepreneur, selling everything from magazines and playing cards to purified water, which I got free from the local pumping station. My father owned his own business as did his brother and father before them, so I came about my entrepreneurial ways in a traditional fashion.

After a period in the Armed Forces, I served an apprenticeship in the automobile business with one of the toughest entrepreneurs I have ever known. At the right moment in time, I opened my first business, a retail contemporary home furnishings and accessories store. Typically, (I'm not recommending this for anyone, but it is a way of beginning I hear about over and over again) I didn't know anything about the business, so I learned fast. In short order, I was quite successful. Through a series of events, I sold out and moved to California, there to really test my abilities in a well-financed venture of my design. Soon, I was heading an organization of thirty retail stores with the usual secretaries, staff, store managers, and workers.

This all culminated just a few years ago at a time when some behavioral scientists were intensively studying entrepreneurs. I was a typical, aggressive entrepreneur on the rise. I had a lot of natural "smarts" and a burning desire to be successful.

Now that I have learned a bit about who I am, what I do, and how I do it, I can look back on my behavior with a great deal of understanding. At the time I was totally unaware of the process of my life. My management style might have been described as that of a benevolent autocrat. I would find young, talented people, pay them extremely well, then expect them to work at the same frenetic pace that I did, and remain loyal. I cared about my people, but I had the first and last say about everything. I was the omnipotent genius who could do no wrong.

It seemed to work. By traditional standards, I appeared to be successful. I had money, traveled first class, and was respected for my ability.

Then it all came unglued. One evening at a party, a woman asked me, "Who are you?" My spontaneous reply was, "I'm a money machine." For weeks that was all I could think about. What was happening with my life? True, I knew how to make money, but what else did I know? How far were my abilities going to carry me? Would the real me, hiding behind the money machine, come out and be seen?

Meanwhile, back at the company, the board of directors, along with a management consultant group, had decided that my entrepreneurial style no longer fitted a multi-million dollar company and that I should be replaced by a corporate style manager. (This is a really important issue and is discussed further in Chapter 17, "Successful Expansion.") Finally, I sold out and went on my way in search of a new business venture.

Well, not quite. I was still haunted by my image of the "money machine" and the notion that I was only partially fulfilling my potential in this life. A friend suggested that a group experience with other business executives who were raising similar questions about their existence might be stimulating. This was the beginning of an adventure that has dramatically altered my value system, my capacity for happiness, my management style, and eventually my life work. Important in the context of this book, the new learnings have enormously increased my productivity and my efficiency as a manager.

THE PROCESS OF PERSONAL GROWTH

My first experience of really relating with a group of people at an intimate level was rewarding beyond belief. I had learned the social norms of our society well—be cool, don't show your emotions, and keep your cover. Shedding some of the layers of my façade and dealing with things as they really are was so exciting that I decided I wanted more—lots more!

Rather than rush back into a business venture, I chose to do some consulting work and to continue looking for the real me. I read everything about growth psychology I could get my hands on. That's when I discovered Carl Rogers, Abraham Maslow, Fritz Perls, and others who have been so important in helping people differentiate between a way of life that is built on how we "should" behave (responding to the environment), as opposed to fulfilling our own real inner needs (responding to ourselves). I also got familiar with contemporary management theory through the writings of Douglas McGregor, Jack Gibb, Chris Argyris, and many more. I found that they were all talking about the same notion of openness, confronting issues, and collaboration.

My next find was Jerry Greenwald and I began regular growth group sessions. Others with me in the group were a nurse, a female advertising executive, a corporate executive, a lawyer, a newly divorced housewife, and a young teacher. Each of us was searching for greater understanding of ourselves and the ability to reach out and communicate more meaningfully with those about us.

As the group work continued and we shared at ever deeper levels, I was astounded at how little I knew about myself. I had been so successful at being "successful" that I almost totally responded to my environment rather than to my own needs. Wild! Here I was, not even knowing how to create my own happiness.

The next learning jolted me even more. I had been taught that to be "manly" was to be strong, not cry, control myself, and, above all, not to show softness. Women in the group began saying how horrible that was. They all wanted a man who was strong, certainly, but who also could be soft and tender and vulnerable. That I could understand, but then it came out that the men also appreciated realness in other men. Out the window with the macho tradition.

This was a lot of stuff for a hard-nosed entrepreneur to assimilate, but I decided to expand my new learnings by joining with other groups. That's when I looked up Carl Rogers' people at La Jolla, California. More groups, more work, more painful insights into my behavior, but each day becoming more open and feeling more free.

I began forming new friends and found myself enjoying just being, not necessarily doing. I was more in contact with nature, I felt full and happy. I was asking directly for what I wanted and rejecting things and people that were not nourishing to me.

One day, I realized that I was a dramatically different person. I was more accepting of people as they are. I could like someone with ideas quite different from my own. My capacity for loving and being loved was greater, and I had developed a deep compassion for, and affinity with, all humanity.

TRANSLATING PERSONAL GROWTH
INTO BUSINESS RESULTS

Then, the fear set in. How could I carry on my life work in the business world and still be this open, caring me? I began to build a philosophical framework for my life that would allow me to have it all. An important cornerstone of this construct is that all the new growth learnings come as an additive process. I decided it was not necessary to drop out or reduce my effectiveness in order to enjoy being more human.

I began to be fully the new me in every activity. As a consultant, I put into practice all my notions about how people like to be together at work. However, being a consultant isn't like being on the firing line. The only way to find out if I could bring it all together was to get back into managerial action again. So, I dusted off a business concept I had worked up a year before and began to form a new company. In the process, I interacted with financial people, formed a corporation, made a lease, developed a merchandising package, purchased goods in the United States and abroad, started to develop a management team—in short, I utilized all the business skills I had learned in my career.

Here's what I found, and *this is the most important thing I have to share with you.* I lost none of the skills I had in dealing with units of production, materials, or any form of "things." But, I had gained a whole new way of dealing successfully with people by simply being me—openly and honestly. Where formerly I had been admired, I was now accepted, cared for, even loved.

I had learned the importance of trust of myself, trust of my people. In this trusting way, I could allow them to be who they are and accept them, opening a space where they could rise to the best that is in them. As a trusting person, I could own up when I made a mistake or didn't know the answer. I could invite and accept helpful feedback from my employees. I could abandon the leader role (I felt good enough about myself that I didn't need this external validation), and I could utilize the decision-making abilities of my team, which I found exceeded my own.

The rest of my story leads up to my present sharing with you. Through a number of happy circumstances, I was invited to teach a university course and later to join the faculty as a full-time professor. I decided to do this as it would give me an opportunity to share my notions about how to make all of one's life a success instead of just the narrow portion we call business. The programs I am assigned to are all at the adult level, and most of my students are in managerial positions. A number are either in their own businesses or moving in that direction. I have had literally hundreds of opportunities to test my management approach through students who have adopted it.

The overwhelming conclusion I have come to is that, for small business owners, technical skill will not suffice. We must become people managers (*not* manipulators), and the path to becoming a successful people manager is through personal growth. As each of us becomes tuned in to who we are, we create the space for others around us to do the same. The result is magical, both in the liberation of each person to realize his own full potential and in the bottom-line profitability of the business.

If you are interested in learning how to communicate better and to grow into success, here are ways you can go about it:

1. Take a laboratory training course. Some sources of lab training are listed at the end of the chapter.

2. Keep a journal. Write in it every day, recording your feelings and thoughts about your interactions with others and about your perceptions of yourself and the world around you. In a few weeks you will begin to notice patterns of behavior that can give you meaningful insight into your life process.

3. Join a growth group. You will be astounded at how many choices there are. Literally hundreds of thousands of Americans are involved in "well people's therapy," seeking to enrich the quality of their lives. These groups are most often run by qualified clinical psychologists. There are many approaches, so check thoroughly to find the right one for you. If you don't feel comfortable in the group of your choice, quit and find another one.

4. Join one of the many leaderless groups, such as those conducted by the TORI Community around the country. Being with others in a community experience, without traditional leaders, is a freeing experience and provides a climate for personal growth that may transcend all others. This concept is best described in the book by Jack Gibb, *Trust: A New View of Personal and Organizational Development*.

5. Read. Try the psychology section of any bookstore and be prepared for a shock. The number of volumes on ways to achieve growth is huge. New books come out every week. Many are already over the million mark in sales. Pick the ones that seem to fit you and then just follow your heart.

6. Meditate. Corporate executives by the thousands are doing it —why not small business owners? Join a class or learn through a book. You may just get insights that will change your life. If nothing else, you will relax and let go of tension, and that may even save your life.

7. Start paying attention to what is going on in your body. All the messages you will ever need are there if you will just tune in. Being in touch with your feelings is a basic path to better communications. You can do some learning by yourself—just take time out from each day to locate feelings in your body. If you want instruction, try a sensory awareness group, practice yoga, work on your energy with a Reichian therapist or a bio-energetic therapist.

Don't forget this original aspect of the personal growth path that is so important: If you grow as a business person, you also grow as a wife, husband, parent, lover, friend. It's all part of the same whole —we're only one person. So, the spin-off is that our lives become enriched with every human contact. We are able to give of ourselves in a total way and to be the recipient of another's totality.

Additional Information

1. Jerry Greenwald. *Be The Person You Were Meant To Be.* Dell Publishing, 1973. (Paperback) Real tools for effectively changing your life style.
2. Carl Rogers. *Carl Rogers On Personal Power.* Delacorte Books, 1977. One of America's most distinguished psychologist's person centered guide to growth and creativity.

3. John Powell. *Why Am I Afraid To Tell You Who I Am?* Argus Communication, 1969. A little paperback with a lot of insights on self-awareness, personal growth, and interpersonal communication.
4. Muriel James and Dorothy Jongeward. *Born To Win.* Addison-Wesley, 1971. (Paperback) Transactional Analysis and Gestalt theory put to work on life decisions.
5. Virginia Satir. *Peoplemaking.* Science and Behavior Books, Inc., 1972. One of America's foremost family therapist's growth guides for the whole family.
6. Association for Humanistic Psychology, 325 Ninth Street, San Francisco, California 94103. Write for a list of growth centers around the United States. You'll be amazed at the variety of places, people and organizations where you can find other souls on the same journey.
7. Learning Resources Corporation, 7594 Eads Avenue, La Jolla, California 92037. This organization conducts seminars and workshops in various parts of the country. Subjects cover all areas of people-managing skills.
8. NTL Institute, P. O. Box 9155, Rosslyn Station, Arlington, Virginia 22209. This is the grandfather of the experiential group business. Write for their catalogue of training groups in many subjects.
9. Jack Gibb. *Trust: A New View Of Personal And Organizational Development.* Guild of Tutors Press, 1978. A whole life theory that will help create your environment the way you want it to be. Perhaps the most important book you can read.

16. MANAGING HUMAN RESOURCES

If there is any one area where entrepreneurs fail as a group, it is in the management of people. It takes an enormous amount of concentrated energy to start a business and nurse it through the first few years. In this formative period, the decision-making emphasis is usually on things and events. This is most unfortunate since people are the most important asset of a business. As one might expect, the mis-direction of attention results in the disintegration of many good partnerships and management teams. In order to correct this major cause of business failure, it is important that the small business owner learn about the management of human resources and re-direct some of his energy.

SMALL BUSINESS AND THE BEHAVIORAL SCIENCES

Working with people is the aspect of management that has drawn the most attention in the past few years from researchers, educators, and organizational consultants. The result is a deluge of monographs, articles, and books on the subject of human behavior in organizations. They point up the obvious: People do not like being treated as units of production. They do not like being rubricized, depersonalized, coerced, or threatened. For the most part, they do not like dull, uninteresting work. They do not like working for authoritarian, unfeeling, autocratic bosses.

The result of old-style management in large corporations shows up in many ways that are unhealthy for our economy. Many young people choose to avoid corporate careers. Productivity is at an all-time low as more and more people fail to find satisfaction at their jobs, draw their pay, and then create the real pleasure of their lives outside the business. Even highly paid executives drop out and turn to alternate lifestyles. The examples of worker dissatisfaction with corporate life go on and on.

What are the real needs and desires of people at work? We don't need to go far from home for answers. Why are you thinking of starting, or why are you already in your own business? When I've asked that question of hundreds of potential or actual entrepreneurs, the answers have centered around the need to be free, to control as much of their own destiny as possible, to find real satisfaction in the work itself, not to be limited to repetitious bits of a job, to have flexibility in the design of the work, and to exercise creativity.

It's not much of a stretch of the imagination to see that if this is what entrepreneurs want out of life, most other people probably want pretty much the same thing. In fact, much of the behavioral research of the past decade confirms that these desires are widely held in the population.

This research information is known to thousands of organizational development specialists and is readily available to thousands of corporate executives. But, to apply corrective measures to work procedures that would release some of the human potential locked up in entrenched bureaucracies is a horrendous undertaking. So, high absenteeism, high turnover, and apathy go on.

The failure of large corporations to utilize the potential of their human resources plays right into the hands of small business. The small business owner does not need to train countless managers and supervisors in good human relations. Smaller size allows him to affect each employee directly. He does not need to work through the endless problems of intergroup relationships and bureaucratic hierarchal levels. He can short-circuit the problems that plague big business and, through the quality of his own presence, make substantial changes in the fit between people and workplace.

The ultimate ability of small business to compete may very well reside in our willingness to learn about and emphasize the human side of enterprise. The goal of attracting and holding workers, and releasing their intrinsic motivation through enrichment of the quality of work life, will surely lead to higher bottom-line profits. Considering that small firms employ over half of the industrial workers in the United States, the results, in terms of the enhancement of human life in our nation, could be rather awesome.

Now that you have waded through all the preliminary rhetoric, let's get down to the business at hand. While it would take eighteen volumes to cover the subject of work-life in larger concerns, I feel safe in attempting a distillation of contemporary behavioral concepts that will suffice for the smaller firm. Study of the material that follows is not guaranteed to gain you entry into that portion of heaven reserved for small-business owners who care about their employees; rather, it is designed to whet your desire to continue your research into improved human-resources management. The basis for all the knowledge you need in order to be a superb manager of people is already within you. All you need do is focus on your own growing.

MOTIVATION

Reward and punishment constituted the motivational method used by managers in the past. Whenever they wanted to move people, they threatened firing or pay reduction. The introduction of unions and the modern welfare system have effectively eliminated most management by threat.

While the stick is useless, the carrot is still very much in vogue, and a whole array of rewards have been designed to prod the worker. If we really study the extrinsic reward system, we find that it is a never-ending affair. Raise someone's pay, and soon they'll want more. Pass out a bonus, and in short order it becomes part of the expectations. Throw a company party at Christmas as a morale booster, and then try to discontinue it. It has become part of the system. Yet we continue to offer the carrots until we are passing them out by the ton.

In reality, most activities are self-motivating. They supply their own intrinsic rewards. People like to work, to be creative, to pull together as a team. People like to see their company succeed and like the deep satisfaction derived from their part in it. But, by constantly offering rewards for those things people already like to do, we change the activity from pleasure to work. The entrepreneur who heavily utilizes the extrinsic reward system is kept constantly busy designing new rewards.

If you want supercharged people, simply capitalize on the intimate nature of small business. Allow the work to remain interesting. Allow people to wear many hats. Let each person play an expanding role in the organization. Don't emulate any of the fragmented jobs big business creates. Pick good people, then get out of their way. You'll have plenty to do guiding the course of the enterprise and you can enjoy being a tension-free person by not being a boss.

Once again, focus on those experiences that brought you to forming your own business. Remember the sense of being owned by your employer? Of not having any say in the conduct of the business? Was there a time when you felt like a puppet, or like an expendable "thing?"

Never forget! Assume that your employees have the same desires that you do. Then, plan your business environment in such a way that those life-contracting, negative conditions never occur.

COLLABORATION

The way to make it all work is to have your organization become one big collaborating team. That means taking the time to have everyone come together as a group. It means confronting conflict. It requires that you be as open and personal as it is possible for you to be with the group and with each member individually. It calls for sharing in many of the basic decisions.

Try this reasoning: You selected the people who work for you. It was completely your choice. If you trust your ability to select, then it is just one more step to allow employees to join in the decision-making process.

If this seems a bit too risky all at once, here's a three step process that works for me:

Stage One—Hand-holding. For new employees, or at the beginning of a new business, I assume a parental role for those who need it. I guide them in a benevolent way, letting them know they can call on me for help and support. I am willing to give them the benefit of my experience, but I *never* order them to do it my way. I encourage them to find a better way if it fits for them. I meet with them frequently, not in the form of checking their work, but only to open the communication between us.

Stage Two—Consultative. When employees are ready to move out of the hand-holding stage (the time frame varies by individuals), I meet with them and let them know that they can do the job without my direction. They are told that I will be available to them when they want to check with me, and that I will feel free to give my advice where appropriate. This phase sets the stage for moving into total collaboration.

Stage Three—Hands off. Not everyone reaches this stage, but if I have done my work well, most will. My assumption now is that Stage Three persons are totally capable of running their own portion of the venture, joining with me and others in a smoothly functioning management team. If something goes awry, it becomes a problem for the whole team.

Using this three-step method keeps me constantly aware of my relationship with each person, allows me to deal with my own trust level as an emerging, rather than forced, process, and confronts the reality that people grow at different rates.

COMMUNICATIONS

In all the literature on people in organizations, the word that comes up most frequently is communication. It's pretty tough to be a good communicator in our society because just about everything we learn works against us. Strong and silent is a virtue. Don't say anything that will hurt anyone. Keep cool and just state the facts. Keep a stiff upper lip. The list goes on and on, and as we respond to these norms, our true, natural selves become covered over with layers of "shoulds" (how we should be and act).

Below all the façades, each of us is an emotional person. We truly want warm personal relationships. We want to express ourselves at a level deeper than the superficial one we usually use. It's fascinating to watch people in group experiences where the norm is changed from superficiality to intimacy. Nearly everyone dives into deep relating rather quickly. We are a nation of people who are starved for meaningful communications, yet few break the barriers and become real.

There are endless publications on the subject of communication. You can find every type of advice imaginable, with charts and diagrams to point the way. You can make a life work out of studying communication. Or, you can short-cut the whole process by just being and showing whoever you are.

Being open means sharing feelings as well as thoughts. It means being congruent—having your outside reflect what is happening on your inside. It means being who you are from moment to moment. Interestingly, in all my experience, openness begets openness. When I am willing to share, others will do the same. Everyone with whom I have worked relates the same experience. Openness may, at first, be difficult to achieve, because you will need to peel away the mistaken learnings of a lifetime, yet many do it. If you elect only one area to work on, try this one. It will take some doing, but the rewards in organizational cohesion and in personal fulfillment are beyond measure.

As a small business owner/manager, the most important contribution you can make to your effectiveness is to become open and straight. This will lead to an organization where no one plays games, where communication is up and lateral, as well as down.

Additional Information

1. Rensis Likert. *The Human Organization.* McGraw-Hill, 1967. A science-based management system, primarily for large corporations. If you sift carefully, there are numerous ideas you can apply to the smaller firm.
2. Douglas McGregor. *The Human Side of Enterprise.* McGraw-Hill, 1960. The classic in the field. An understanding of theory X and Y will give you a real base for your own activities.
3. Frederick Herzberg. *Work and The Nature of Man.* World, 1968. (Paperback) Job enrichment and its effect on productivity.
4. E. F. Schumacher. *Small is Beautiful: Economics As If People Mattered.* Harper and Row, 1973. (Paperback) If you want to get a perspective on small business around the world, this is important reading. Schumacher was the leader in futuristic thinking about appropriate technology.
5. Sidney Jourard. *Transparent Self.* Van Nostrand Reinhold, 1971. An existential psychologist focuses on self-disclosure.

17. SUCCESSFUL EXPANSION

As a young company evolves and shows a success pattern, the question of expansion arises. Sometimes there is no choice, as with a product that requires improvement of market position in order to remain competitive. Most often, growth is a matter of choice and a thorough examination of the firm is undertaken to assist the go, no-go decision. Advantages may be explored such as increased profitability, security in the market place, new challenges, new opportunities for the employees. Disadvantages explored may include the cash drain, growing impersonality, loss of advantage of smallness, risks of increased overhead. What is usually *not* explored are all the issues surrounding the entrepreneur himself and the problems that go with his changing role.

THE ENTREPRENEURIAL DILEMMA

There have been a variety of studies done on the nature of entrepreneurs. Several threads run throughout all of them.

1. Entrepreneurs tend to be realists. They see the world the way it is and try to make a place for themselves in it. They would probably not expend their energy being reformers.

2. They are innovative. Opportunities are seen and taken. They jump in and make things happen.

3. The most universal characteristic of entrepreneurs is a never-ending sense of urgency.

4. The need to control and direct is both the great strength and the great weakness of entrepreneurs. The impulsive "taking-charge" is the basic stuff of which new ventures are made. It may also keep entrepreneurs from making the transition to successful managers. The essence of successful management is being a people manager, and compulsive authoritarian control does not produce positive results in larger organizations.

A number of management experts see entrepreneurs as good for start-ups but never transitioning to successful managers. They would have the entrepreneur step down and turn the business over to professional managers at a certain point in the venture's growth. The problem is that firmly entrenched entrepreneurs don't step down—they rarely consider the possibility. Therein lies the entrepreneurial dilemma—how to maximize those strengths and abilities that get ventures started, letting go of none of that energy, but adding new dimensions that will optimize management potential.

FROM "FLAIR AND HUNCH" TO MANAGEMENT

Becoming aware of the dilemma is the first step on the transition road. Most small business persons move blithefully along using a modified business plan to guide their expansion, without once taking an inward look at their own readiness. The first question to ask is, "Do I really want to do this?" Many of us respond to a lifetime of learnings about how we "should" be, rather than to our own needs. Being out of touch with yourself at this point can lead to personal and financial catastrophe, not only for you but for a growing number of employees who depend on the business for their livelihoods.

In my class for aspiring entrepreneurs I devote a session to creative career planning. The objective is for each person to have an in-depth look at his own motivation and what he really wants out of his business life. You might wish to try some of these exercises.

1. Head a sheet of paper, "Who Am I?" Try to answer this question twenty ways, using phrases which describe you most accurately in regard to your career.

2. Go back over your list and mark each one "+" (positive), "-" (negative) or "0" (neutral) based on how you feel about this trait or description.

3. Go over the list once more. Assign a rank to each item from one to twenty, with number one being the concept or description

most central to your existence. A good way to do this is to start with the least important first, working backwards until you have the parts of you that are most important to your identity.

4. Take another sheet of paper. Head it, "Where Do I Want To Be?" Answer this ten ways regarding your career. Be as free as possible in selecting the ten goals. For example: I want to be president of a public corporation. Then assign a priority value to each of your career goals. Use this four-point scale and assign the appropriate value to each.

1—of little importance
2—of moderate importance
3—of great inportance
4—of very great importance

5. Take another sheet. Head it, "My Three Priority Goals." From your list of goals, select the three most important. With these goals in mind, answer the questions:

a. What are my strengths and weaknesses affecting my ability to achieve these goals?
b. What obstacles are to prevent me from achieving these goals?
c. Are these goals realistic? What will happen if I do not achieve these goals?

This may appear like a simple set of exercises, but it has some rather profound implications. I have had executives, midway into an expansion move, discover they were following a path they had set early in their careers; but the new path they *really* desired led to the old fishing hole.

Assuming that you really are ready, what are the processes of transitioning from entrepreneur to manager? The first is giving up control. As the business expands, you will need to delegate both responsibility and authority. Coupled with this is the building of an organization and the development of a management team. As discussed in an earlier chapter, this is mainly a process of personal growth. It becomes a matter of trust in your own internal processes and in the capabilities of your people. Poor supervisory practices may be tolerable when a business is small, but expansion demands a deep understanding of people and the ability to work with them.

There are a variety of ways to begin your development of managerial skills. One good way is through reading some of the extensive literature on this subject. A growing number of people find this the right time in their careers and lives to update their education. The university at which I teach offers an MBA for presidents and key executives, and one-third of this program is devoted to the behavioral (people) area. Schools around the country have similar adult programs. Whichever growth method you choose, it is clear that if you are going to expand the business you also need to expand yourself.

SHIFTING RELATIONSHIPS

In the very small enterprise, the owner is often the personification of the firm. Interface with employees is constant and personal. Problems are surfaced and handled simply because there is no place to hide.

In the expanding firm, the owner can no longer handle the growing number of people, so he hires new managers, works them into a team, and delegates authority. As communication shifts from the owner to new executives, old employees tend to get resentful. Information comes to the chief executive on a more formalized basis, and many problems begin.

The entrepreneurial way is to switch hats, run out into the plant or the store, and get involved. The aware, transitioning executive will recognize this peril and work through his management team.

NOT TOO FAST

Put yourself into this scenario: The growth program is underway. Things are booming, and profits are excellent. You become infatuated with your own talent and begin to expand rapidly in many directions. You acquire another business, dabble in real estate, back an invention. All of these require different talents than the one in which you made your success. You're not sleeping so well as you try to stretch your understanding to meet your new involvements . . .

Now try the re-written scenario: You expand your business in steps as you expand your own capabilities. You examine your strengths and learn how to play them. You are aware of your weaknesses and hire capable people to take over where you leave off. You're never complacent, and you continue to innovate. You reach to your limit, but not beyond.

For the entrepreneur in transition to manager, the psychological adjustment is difficult. The path is strewn with bodies. Very few make it, but it can be done.

Additional Information

1. Orvis F. Collins and David G. Moore. *The Organization Makers: A Behavioral Study of Independent Entrepreneurs.* Appleton-Century-Crofts, 1970. A re-write, for the layman, of the authors' 1964 research project. Studies a substantial number of entrepreneurs, their social and work history.
2. David McClelland and David Burnham. *Power Is The Great Motivator. Harvard Business Review,* volume 54, number 2 (March, 1976), pp. 100–110. Clearly differentiates the power motivation of corporate managers and the achievement motivation of entrepreneurs.
3. Abraham Maslow. *Eupsychian Management.* Richard D. Irwin, Inc. and The Dorsey Press, 1965. The father of humanistic psychology speaks to humanistic management.
4. Nena O'Neill and George O'Neill. *Shifting Gears.* Avon Books, 1974. About crucial changes in yourself and your relationships in a changing world.
5. Gail Sheehy. *Passages.* Bantam Books, 1977. (Paperback) Read this before you begin any expansion.
6. Meyer Friedman and Ray Rosenman. *Type A Behavior And Your Heart.* Fawcett Publications, 1975. (Paperback) Read this and re-examine your physical well-being before you expand.

18. SMALL BUSINESS OF THE FUTURE

There are two parts to a discussion of the future of small business: What is the broad economic outlook for small business? How will small businesses of the future integrate personal fulfillment and economic viability?

SMALL BUSINESS AND THE AMERICAN ECONOMY

Apart from the new humanism of small enterprise, the implications of smallness to the international economic order are now coming under study. Owing to the late British economist, E. F. Schumacher, and his book, *Small Is Beautiful,* new consideration is being given to "appropriate technology." Schumacher argued that high technology is inappropriate in many situations. What is often needed is technology that will employ great numbers of people, use less of scarce resources, and serve the human person instead of making him the servant of machines. The use of ample labor rather than scarce resources and job-reducing high technology in an emerging nation, for example, makes obvious sense. Similarly, appropriate technology, coupled with new small-business ventures, might solve some of the continuing high unemployment problems we face right here at home.

If there were fewer restrictions on small enterprise, more people would create their own jobs rather than depend on large corporate employers to offer them work. PL 94–305 directed *The Study of Small Business,* prepared by the Office of Advocacy, U. S. Small Business Administration. It makes a number of recommendations to Congress, including making loans easier to obtain, easing the tax burden, reducing government paperwork, and providing increased management assistance. Many of these recommendations are now under study. Considering that small business employs more than one-half the nation's work force, provides 43 per cent of the national product and 48 per cent of the nation's gross business product,[1] it is certain that this vital sector of the economy will get new and revitalized government support in the years to come.

SMALL BUSINESS AS A WAY OF LIFE

By its very nature, small business operates in relatively personal ways. It fosters intimacy while larger organizations foster remoteness and alienation. It is the vehicle for artists, entertainers, musicians. Just as owning one's own business was the great American economic dream of years gone by, today a small business provides a way for Americans to get free of the stifling overbigness of corporate life.

Following are two operational examples of new ventures that are striving to realize their potential for both profit and self-fulfillment.

Bee Yourself

Marcy, Don and their son live in the suburbs of a large metropolitan area. They are in the process of transitioning from a large multi-national corporation to a new life-style. One evening I visited with them in their home. This is a verbatim transcript from a tape recording of our conversation.

Byron: Don, I'm really intrigued by the new bee supply store that you and Marcy have just started. Before we get into the business itself, I'd like to know about your background.

Don: My background is in business administration—mostly with one company—nineteen years with _____ Company. For the past five years, I've been a manager. The pay is okay, and it's certainly secure, but I've come to

[1]Office of Advocacy, U. S. Small Business Administration. *The Study of Small Business,* 1977, p. 13.

the point lately where I see the cast of characters changing with the work remaining pretty much the same. I'm seeing twenty more years of repetition and, at 38, that's not very exciting.

Byron: Is what you're saying that there's no challenge?

Don: Recently, it has come down to that. For a while, I was expanding personally and moving up the hierarchy; but the last few years the challenge is gone, and I'm finding the company more stifling. I've been lucky being at a smaller location where I have more to do, but I'm subject to transfer back to a bigger location and then the scope of my work becomes narrow.

Byron: So, you are always faced with being squeezed into a box, even at the managerial level?

Don: Yes, I'm as far as I can go at this location, and the next move is more constricting. I'm really not willing to do that.

Byron: I hear this so often in my conversations with corporate managers. The experience they relate is like having the life squeezed out of them.

Don: That's true. In the last few years, I've become aware of myself and my potential. Through some growth group work, I've learned that there's more to my work life than what's happening. Actually, Marcy beat me to it. She realized her need to grow first and got involved in a growth seminar. It's tougher for a man to get started, I think. We have this big male ego involved. The other thing I did was start back to school. That's been a real eye-opener. I've had some significant awakenings as a result of that experience. I'm seeing that there's a lot out there one can do if one is willing.

Byron: Where did the small business enter the picture?

Don: We'd been talking about a business of our own fairly seriously the past few months—probably the discussions go back a couple of years. It was really Marcy's wanting out of the rat race and into her own thing.

Byron: Want to get into the conversation here, Marcy?

Marcy: I started out being a teacher, and as I look back on it, it was quite fulfilling but low-paying. I was still in college, and a job came along that paid well, with a big company. I wanted money, so I took it.

And I wound up in the traditional female job, typing and filing. Even then, I resented it. That led to more of the same, and eventually I got into the same company that Don is in. I've worked there thirteen years. I started as a receptionist. I wound up doing a variety of work, but it was at a sort of receptionist level. It was okay until I got transferred into one of those box-like jobs. I found I simply couldn't do it and asked for a transfer to dispatching, which turned out okay.

Byron: What finally happened with your job?

Marcy: It went up and down—sometimes okay, but most often stifling. I finally realized that there was this rage going on inside of me because I couldn't do what I wanted to do. I hadn't realized that one could really choose. When I discovered this, I said to myself that I simply didn't have to do this kind of work if I didn't want to.

Byron: Is there any part of this that has to do with the feminine aspects—did you get held down because you were a woman?

Marcy: Part of it is because I let myself fall into the typing thing. But in school I wouldn't take typing because it felt wrong. It really became a matter of survival. It was all I could do, so I did it; and I did it for many years. Finally, my job was dissolved and I got a temporary assignment to set up a library for the company. I didn't know anything about libraries, but no one else did either, so they let me alone. Well, I set up the library, and I learned that I could do a lot of things if I wanted to. After that, it was back to the boring grind. I really resented it when they told me I should be happy I had a job.

Byron: How did the business enter in? Did you go actively looking for a small business?

Marcy: Not at all.

Byron: How did it happen?

Marcy: It was very strange—it was more like an experience. I don't even know if I can describe it for you. It was just a willingness—something I had put out there in the universe that I wanted to do. I didn't actively seek any particular business.

Byron: It sounds like you were seeking a business.

Marcy: No, I was really seeking a change in my life.

Byron: Okay, I understand.

Marcy: Well, I guess I had a notion that it would be a small business of my own. Anyhow, I was having lunch with a friend, and she told me that a small store was for sale in the neighborhood. It sold honey and bee supplies. I got in contact with the owner and found out it was small enough for us to handle. Somehow it made sense, and I was able to let go of all the barriers I had going on inside me.

Byron: You were totally dissatisfied with your life work.

Marcy: Yes, it was a total unwillingness to play the game anymore.

Byron: The game?

Marcy: I saw that there was a game going on out there, and I had a sense of what the game was and I didn't like the way it was set up. I wanted to set up my own game. When this thing came up, it made sense—and at the same time it didn't have any sense to it at all. I wasn't afraid of it. I think Don was more afriad than I was.

Don: Yes, I'd been aware of Marcy's frustration for a couple of years. And, off and one, we talked about a business. I was still willing to play the game until just a few months ago. When this opportunity came up, I was ready. We didn't know the first thing about bees or honey, but we looked into it anyhow. We got the financial records. There wasn't much there, but the more we looked, the more intrigued we got.

Byron: How did the transaction go?

Don: We did all the dumb things. We didn't go to an attorney or an accountant. The business had been going for a year and a half and growing quite steadily. There wasn't any competition around. We went into it more with our guts than anything else. It just had a good feeling for us.

Byron: There are all types of businesses. Others didn't attract you, but this one did. What was there about it?

Marcy: It was small. It was where we liked living. And the whole story of bees turned out to be fascinating. Lots of people work with bees as a hobby, and it turns out they're very genuine.

Byron: You spoke to customers at the store? What were they like?

Marcy: You'd never know what they did for a living. There's a real honesty about them. I found myself experiencing people for people. I always thought of myself as selective and not liking many people. Now that I'm in this business, I experience a real love for people just because they are who they are. These beekeepers—there's something about a total willingness to let the bees be who they are and to experience the social creature that the bee is. Even experts in the field will own that they don't know all there is to know about bees. I like that. It's so exciting to be part of something that's an ongoing process.

Byron: Your customers are hobbyists, not professionals?

Marcy: Right, just hobbyists. There are all types—doctors, office workers, housewives.

Byron: What changes has owning the business made in your life? You've already mentioned the behavioral change—coming to like people more.

Marcy: One of the things I'm learning is that I want to *have* the business, not become the business. I don't have my survival wrapped up in this. I want to enjoy it. It's a total willingness to be there.

Byron: Isn't part of it an economic plan?

Marcy: In a sense, but we're willing to let that evolve. We're not into efforting. I feel good when we make a lot of money, but that's not everything. Part of it is not setting up huge expectations.

Byron: Are you happier now than when you were working for the corporation?

Marcy: Yes. I would like to expand the business a bit. It's very small. Don does the books—he enjoys that.

Don: When we started, my role was going to be supportive; and I was going to continue on with my job. A few days after we started, it was like getting hit on the head with a sledge hammer. We realized how naive we were—we knew nothing. So we started reading everything we would get our hands on regarding beekeeping. We both signed up for courses in beekeeping. In a short time, we gained some confidence and began talking to customers like experts.

Byron: Sounds like you're enjoying your part.

Don: More than that. It's a real release for me. I can escape from being an administrator and get into bees. Some of the things that are happening are amazing. We started catching and selling swarms, which is a trip.

Marcy: When we bought the business, the owners really wanted to sell, but they couldn't understand how we could buy it without knowing something about the business. They couldn't understand that we weren't intimidated. There are so many things we all can do. Just because we haven't done it before doesn't mean anything. We have the capability to do incredible things.

Byron: Can we discuss some of the financial aspects?

Marcy: Surely. We've made the business grow. While we're still learning technically, we feel we're better managers than the former owners. We're now looking into how to expand the lines so we can handle more items that are compatible with honey.

Don: It's a seasonal business—heavy in spring. Our sales generally have exceeded our expectations. We want to level them out.

Marcy: In about a year, we expect the business earnings to be paying out as much or more than I made on my job.

Byron: You're saying that the rewards come from several places —the nature of the business itself and the sense of accomplishment. You'll really like it even better as it pays off.

Marcy: There's the total responsibility, too. It's all up to us. I enjoy that. It's a great feeling not to have anyone behind me.

Byron: So, it's worth the year's sacrifice of earnings to get the business started?

Marcy: Absolutely. Before, it was empty money. Our priorities are changing. When I write a check now, I realize the value of money. I'm more involved with the nature of the money.

Byron: Let me take you on a new track. Looking ahead, what are your fantasies about the business? What would you like to see happen?

Marcy: I think we can be as totally outrageous in our thinking as we wish. I use the term "outrageous" because there are no limitations on what can be accomplished. We've talked about the possibility that we can expand. Don loves it. Perhaps he'll run with it, and I'll do something else.

Byron: Marcy, you're saying that for you the business has a very personal value, not a monetary value. What's it for you, Don?

Don: I'm from a small town, and I always wanted to be a successful businessman. My life has been goal-oriented. I've set timetables for my life, and I've met most of them. That's really been running my life until we got into this thing. What this business has really done for me is let me know that I can make a living and have fun. I'd gotten to the point where I wasn't having fun anymore. I don't know which direction it will go, but we're now looking into allied businesses. We're checking organic farming and natural foods. We have thoughts about inviting young people in to explore beekeeping and things like that. No clear direction. Just lots of excitement.

Marcy: Part of that scares me. I want a small business with a lid on it—and without a lid on it. I don't want it to run me like the corporation did.

Don: I want it to keep being fun. When it stops being that, I want out of it.

Byron: Has being in this together made a difference in your relationship?

Don: Very definitely. Before, we lived the corporation. Now, we live our own thing. Our priorities are changing. We're meeting different people, and our communication is better.

Marcy: There's a freshness to our relationship. Don always had an appreciation for me, but he could never see the depth of me as a person. We were feeding off old stuff. It was clear to me I had to reach out for more of me.

Don: Yes, I could see her frustration, but as a well indoctrinated manager I was usually spouting the corporate line. Things have changed with our being together in the business.

Byron: You're both very much the embodiment of my version of the new entrepreneur.

Don: I think that the concept of success/failure has to be looked at in a new way. Really, it has to do with inner satisfaction; and this is what we are reaching for.

Life Transitions

This is a three-person partnership, set up to conduct seminars, create documentaries, and write books on various life transitions. Its initial activity is a program to assist people who want to change careers. Persons entering the program begin by putting their past lives into perspective so they can recognize patterns and avoid repeating mistakes. Next, they work on understanding where they want to go. This is all done in a supportive group context. Finally, they are provided with the tools that will help them get what they want. As you might imagine, a substantial number find their way into businesses of their own.

Several things are unique about this business. Several years ago it would have had no basis for existence. Very few people attempted career changes because once they had established themselves in an industry they were labeled, and the only job changes available were moves within the same occupation. But, with the shift in consciousness, more and more people are searching for a fulfilling life. For many that means entirely new work. Recent studies indicate that over half of the management people in American industry are considering changing careers. So, a new business has been created to help people who want a new business.

The philosophy and management style of the principals is a model of how totally rewarding small-business life can be. *Life Transitions* is a profit-making organization and bottom line results are always in focus; but of equal importance are the personal growth and career expansion of the group members.

The organization has no offices, no titles, and no specifically designated jobs. All decisions are made by the group. Each person is capable of performing all the functions of the organization, and workloads are shared on a time available basis.

Unlike the usual tightly structured business meetings, those of *Life Transitions* proceed in an open, high trust, organic way. Intrapersonal and interpersonal conflicts have a high priority on the group's time. Problems are not buried or allowed to simmer—they are surfaced and worked. Consideration is given to the personal needs of each member, and the organizational goals are constantly modified to fit them.

By traditional management standards, this is a peculiar business indeed. Imagine trying to integrate business activities into the total life flow of the participants. Unheard of, time consuming, not a productive business activity.

Wrong! On close inspection, what makes this model really exciting is that the integration of traditional business goals with individual life goals releases a tremendous flow of energy that becomes available to the clients. In a service business, satisfied clients means high bottom-line profits. Once more, the circle closes.

SMALL BUSINESS AS A FORCE FOR CHANGE

This is my fantasy of the future.

Phase I

As disenchantment with the quality of work life in large corporations and government bureaucracies grows, ever increasing numbers of women and men drop out to begin small businesses of their own. Their primary motivation is to get free and live a life of total fulfillment. Revamped tax laws now allow small ventures to retain more profits, and this increased economic viability adds to the attractiveness. Big business and big government recognize the trend and across the country it is the discussion subject in meetings of organizational leaders.

Many of the new business owners prefer the simple life of less densely populated regions and they resettle in smaller communities. This substantial emigration begins to reduce the problems of urban centers. Large organizations feel the pinch as jobs become hard to fill.

Phase II

Big business is still talking about making the work environment more desirable. Thousands of meetings and thousands of consultants later they have not been able to make any plans to stem the tide. Workers continue to leave in substantial numbers.

With their new consciousness and re-awakened creativity the small business owners have made substantial dents in the sales and profits of big business. As their need for employees increases, the big companies frantically increase salaries. This adds to product costs until one day their technological advantage over small business disappears. Without a price advantage, big business loses its last appeal.

New research studies on small business owners and their employees show that these people tend to live longer and have less incidents of stress diseases, particularly heart attacks and cancer, than their counterparts in big industry.

Phase III

Corporate executives fall into disrepute. They are replaced in high government positions by small business women and men who systematically begin to dismantle big government and set up local town-hall meetings. Since small business is highly labor-intensive, unemployment has disappeared. All the ex-government employees easily find jobs; and there is no further need for welfare.

Elsewhere in the industrial world, similar events are taking place. As the giant machinery of the world falls into disrepair, no one is able to produce weapons of war.

Many years ago the bureaucrats who were advising the less advantaged nations were replaced by small business persons who helped them dispose of their heavy machinery and apply appropriate technology. They have advanced rapidly and, no longer in need of financial assistance, have taken an equal place in the world.

Small business owners have taken over the United Nations. Since their natural way is to be open and direct, diplomatic game-playing has been eliminated. Personal invective has been replaced by collaboration, and nationalism has now become internationalism.

Now that multi-national corporations have disappeared, world business is conducted amicably and without resort to threats and bribery. Since there is no one to run the giant computers, people once again talk to each other. Everywhere there is peace and harmony and love. . . . .

Acknowledgments

This book was originally scheduled for one of the large publishers. When it took two months for them to answer a letter and two weeks to answer a phone call, I had second thoughts. In my own life I want to be free of large dehumanizing organizations. Happily, I got together with Paul Proehl and the Guild of Tutors Press. Small *is* beautiful. Imagine having the president of the company for your very own editor. Thanks, Paul. I am really grateful for all your help.

To Dick Rierdan and Annette Fuchs, my associates, thanks for putting up with me and allowing me to cop out on my work with you while I finished this book.

Barbara Carlstein read and encouraged me from the first page. Ida Fisher really believes in me, and that works better than chicken soup when I am down.

Thanks to all of my wonderful students who let me babble on about my visions of the way the world can be, and then gave me feedback that clarified the whole thing.

The real partner in this operation is smiling, lovely JoAnn Medora, who typed the manuscript from tapes and chicken-scratched pieces of paper, and never complained—not even once.

Special thanks for their excellent photographic contributions go to Holly Hartman and V. M. Robertson. Their pictures of new entrepreneurs who have freed themselves help make the book.

My daughter, Janet, and I are proud of each other, and her special love does wonderful things for my energy.

Byron D. Lane

Index of Photographs

The chapter-heading photographs, listed by page number, are by Holly Hartman of San Francisco and V. M. Robertson of San Mateo, California. The women and men pictured are representative of the new entrepreneur. All cities are in California.

12—Come Fly a Kite, Inc., San Francisco—Dinesh Bahadur.

24—PST, Sausalito—Pierre Pelet.

41—Creative Knits, San Mateo—Ruth and Clifton Nevatt.

46—Del Puerto Data, Inc., Modesto—Stephen Bryant.

52—BAS Designs, Corte Madera—Susan and Brian Anuskewicz.

62—Ladera Garden Center, Menlo Park—Dan Poiree.

68—Liberty Lady Locksmith, San Francisco—Gwendolyn Thibodeaux.

74—Wonder Woman Electric, San Francisco—Susanne Vincenza Sylvia Israel, Val Ramirez, Molly Martin, and Patricia Manns.

84—Greta Alexander, Jeweler, San Francisco.

100—Western Typography, San Francisco—Albrecht Hercules.

108—Rick Fanthorpe-White, Graphic Design and Photography, San Francisco.

119—Pyro Sol, Inc., Redwood City—James Welty.

124—The Naturalist Bookstore, Menlo Park—Edward Haynes.

129—Van Ginkel & Moor, San Francisco.

138—Music Man Mobile Disco, San Francisco—Andrew R. Ebon.

147—Ed Mock Dance Studio, San Francisco—Ed Mock.

154—St. Tropez Hair Design for Men and Women, San Francisco—Phyllis Jong and Maurice Cohen.

160—Olivia Records, San Francisco—Michelle Clinton, Robin Brooks, and Liz Brown.